STUDY GUIDE

for
Modern Real Estate Practice

FOURTEENTH EDITION

This publication is designed to provide accurate and authoritative information in regard to the subject matter covered. It is sold with the understanding that a publisher is not engaged in rendering legal, accounting or other professional service. If legal advice or other expert assistance is required, the services of a competent professional person should be sought.

Publisher: Carol Luitjens
Senior Real Estate Writer: Evan M. Butterfield
Project Manager: Ron Liszkowski
Project Editor: Margaret Haywood

Published by Real Estate Education Company®,
a division of Dearborn Financial Publishing, Inc.®
155 North Wacker Drive
Chicago, Illinois 60606-1719
(312) 836-4400
http:\\www.real-estate-ed.com

Printed in the United States of America.

97 98 10 9 8 7 6 5 4 3 2

Contents

Preface

Most students find their real estate principles class to be a challenging, rewarding and traumatic experience, all at the same time. For some, mastering the basic jargon of the real estate industry can be as demanding as learning a foreign language. Students who have not attended classes or studied for exams for several years sometimes find it difficult to get back into the habit—particularly when they have other important demands on their time, and homework is just another responsibility among many. Real Estate Education Company is aware of the particular challenges that face today's real estate students. This *Study Guide for Modern Real Estate Practice* was written with your needs in mind.

About This Book

This *Study Guide* is designed to be used in conjunction with *Modern Real Estate Practice*, 14th Edition, by Galaty, Allaway and Kyle. It can also be used with the various state supplements, including the state "Practice & Law" series. Each chapter in the *Study Guide* corresponds to a chapter in the main text.

The *Study Guide* is intended to reinforce and elaborate on the basic information provided in *Modern Real Estate Practice*. Specifically, it is designed to help you master the three fundamental goals that are vital to academic success:

1. **Study** and review important concepts;
2. **Evaluate** your understanding of basic real estate issues; and
3. **Apply** learned principles to real-world practice.

These goals form the basis for the basic **learning objectives** of the *Study Guide for Modern Real Estate Practice*:

- *define and explain* fundamental concepts and vocabulary terms of the real estate industry
- *identify and understand* the characteristics of various legal and financial relationships involved in a real estate transaction
- *perform* basic financial and property-related calculations

To help you along the way, this *Study Guide* uses several different learning strategies: an approach called **multitesting**. Each of the styles of self-testing included here has been proven effective in helping students not only memorize factual information, but actually retain the material in a constructive way. By working through the various components of each chapter, you will be reinforcing your real estate knowledge as well as your test-taking skills.

Why a Multitesting Approach?

The advantage of the multitesting approach is that the same material is tested repeatedly, but in different styles. While the real estate examination itself is exclusively multiple-choice, the use of other testing styles helps reinforce your understanding of the subject matter. The stronger your basic understanding, the more prepared you'll be for possible exam curveballs.

NOTE! *This* **Study Guide** *is* **_NOT_** *a substitute for attending class or reading the main text! It's a tool to help you understand and retain what you've learned and read.*

Before You Start . . .

This Preface includes complete instructions for all the exercises contained in the *Study Guide*. You may refer to these instructions at any time as you work through the various problem sections of each chapter. In addition, the instructions include **Study Strategies**: tips and tools you can use to make the *Study Guide* exercises as effective as possible.

The **Math Quick-Review** chart is designed to help students who need a little extra work on their real estate and financial calculation skills. It will direct you to the specific questions throughout the *Study Guide* that address various math applications. With the Quick-Review chart, you can give yourself a complete math skills test and identify those areas that require further study. A list of suggested study materials is included.

Acknowledgments

The following individuals provided invaluable professional guidance and real-world expertise in the development of this *Study Guide*:

- **DEBORAH ASHBROOK, DREI** — *Coldwell Banker Mid-America Group School of Real Estate*
- **LINDA A. EDWARDS** — *Champion Realty, Inc.*
- **RICHARD S. LINKEMER, DREI** — *American School of Real Estate, Ltd.*
- **WALT MCLAUGHLIN** — *Director, McColly School of REALTORS®*
- **THOMAS L. MEYER** — *Cape Girardeau Missouri School of Real Estate*
- **PAUL F. WILKINSON, CRS** — *Long & Foster Institute of Real Estate*
- **DON W. WILLIAMS** — *Alabama Courses in Real Estate*

Instructions

How To Use the *Study Guide*

Each chapter in this *Study Guide* includes the following sections:

Chapter Summary A general summary of the chapter's contents, but with a difference: key terms and important concepts have been replaced by blanks for you to fill in.

■■■■■ **STUDY STRATEGY:** First try to fill in the blanks from memory, without referring to the main text. This self-test will help you discover just how much of the reading you've retained and what information you might need to review.

Key Term Matching Test yourself to see how many of the key terms and other important real estate words you can match with their correct definitions. In some chapters, we've split this section into two parts to make it easier for you to use. Each part is completely self-contained. Simply write the number of the definition in the blank next to the correct key term.

■■■■■ **STUDY STRATEGY:** If you don't know, don't guess! One purpose of this *Study Guide* is to help you find out what you need to read again. Guessing may make it seem like you understand more than you really do.

True and False This section presents a series of statements based on material in the main text. You have two jobs: (1) identify whether the statement is true or false, and (2) revise any false statements so they are true. First, write "True" or "False" (or "T" or "F," or "Yes" or "No") in the blank next to each statement. If the statement is true, go on; if it's false, rewrite it in the space provided at the end of the exercise, making it true.

■■■■■ **STUDY STRATEGY:** Be careful! These statements are designed to test how closely you can read, and how clearly you understand what you've read: they may be tricky. When you rewrite a false statement, you should usually try to change only a few key words: keep the statement's main topic intact. *Don't worry if your revised answer is not word-for-word exactly as printed in the answer key*: the goal is to state the basic idea correctly.

Here's an example:

　　　　14. **A real estate appraiser is licensed by the state to buy, sell, rent or lease real property.**

The statement is clearly *False*. At the end of the section, you write:

14. Real estate brokers are licensed by the state to buy, sell, rent or lease real property.

In the Answer Key, you would find:

14. *False* **A real estate *broker* is licensed by the state to buy, sell, rent or lease real property.**

The focus of the question is clearly on the *characteristics of a real estate broker*. Your answer is correct. Of course, rewriting the statement to define an appraiser would also be correct, but it would involve extra work on your part. The better choice is to stick to the question's main idea. As a rule, the smaller the changes you have to make to create a true statement, the better. In this example, changing only one word made the statement true.

Multiple Choice Review
Each chapter of the main text includes a section of multiple-choice questions. Here you are presented with some additional multiple choice problems. This format helps you retain information as well as prepare for the format and structure of the licensing exam.

■ **STUDY STRATEGY:** Again, don't guess! While "educated guessing" may be useful on the licensing exam where every correct answer counts, your purpose here is to work toward comprehension.

Illustrations
One way people remember information is through pictures. In these sections, you are asked to complete an illustration of one or more basic concepts. Some of the illustrations are reproduced from the main text, while most have been created especially for this *Study Guide*. Some illustrations ask you simply to label certain elements; for others, you may need to analyze information and fill in a practice-related form.

■ **STUDY STRATEGY:** Try to visualize the concepts presented in the illustrations. Quickly filling in the blanks will not help you create a useful mental picture.

Answer Key

Finally, the *Study Guide* includes a complete set of answers at the back of the book.

Don't look at the answers until you've completed all the sections in the chapter! If you check your answers after each section, you might accidentally peek at the correct responses for the next section. While that might improve your overall scores in the *Study Guide*, it won't help your score where it counts: on the licensing exam.

At the end of each chapter, look for the **Answer Key icon**. It will tell you the page in the Answer Key where you can find that chapter's correct responses.

Each chapter in the Answer Key is separated by an easy-to-spot 3-bar **Chapter Tab** that makes it a simple matter to find the answers.

Final Hints

■ *Write in this book!*

■ When working on a complicated fact-pattern problem (whether in this *Study Guide* or on the real estate licensing examination), *draw a picture*. Make a chart or diagram of the transactions involved in the problem. Label each actor by identifier and illustrate the role he or she plays in the event. For instance, if the problem is "*F* conveyed Blueacre to *G*, who conveyed a life estate pur autre vie to *H*, measured by the life of *Y*, retaining a reversionary interest," you might draw a diagram like this:

■ When you're faced with a math problem, *read the whole question carefully!* Sometimes testers (and even this *Study Guide*) will include distracting or irrelevant facts or numbers, to make sure you know not only *how* to perform certain calculations, but know what information you need to do it. For example, if a question wants you to calculate a broker's commission on a sale, you can disregard information about the asking price or mortgage.

■ *Never assume!* You should be able to answer a question based only on the facts you're given. Be sure to pay attention to what you're really being asked to do. Don't make the mistake of answering a question that isn't really being asked.

Math *Quick-Review*

Looking for a quick review of some real estate math principles? Use the following chart to locate the questions in this *Study Guide* that ask you to perform real estate math calculations. The page reference given is for the chapter's first math question.While this book is not intended to offer a thorough math review, working through the math questions will help you focus on problem areas for further study.

TOPIC	CHAPTER	QUESTIONS	PAGE
appraisal	18	1, 2, 6, 9, 11	147
capital gains	3	9, 11	18
commercial leases	16	Figure 16.1	134
commissions (calculating percentages)	6	1, 3, 5, 8, 10	44
commissions, rent per square unit	17	4, 5	139
commissions (calculating compensation)	5	8, 10	37
conveyance of jointly owned property	8	6	67
cost per square unit, calculating size	9	1, 2, 3, 4, 9, 12	73
homestead exemptions	7	10	57
mortgage types, payments, P&I	15	Figure 15.1	126
payments per month	15	9	121
points, percentages, foreclosure	14	2, 6, 10	114
principal and interest	15	1, 4, 5, 6, 7, 9	123
proration, credit/debit	22	1 - 5, 12 - 14	179
real estate taxes	10	4	82
sales contract calculations	11	Figure 11.1	92
sample settlement statement	22	Figure 22.1	182
transfer tax	12	10, 11	100

1 Introduction to the Real Estate Industry

Chapter Summary

1. In general, the most widely recognized real estate activity is _____.

2. Only members of NAR are entitled to be known as _____.

3. The five types of real property classifications are:

   _____, _____,

   _____, _____

   and _____.

4. A _____ is a place where goods and services can

   be bought and sold and price levels established.

5. Because of its unique features, real estate is relatively slow to adjust to the two

   forces of _____ and _____.

Key Term Matching

1. A place where goods can be bought and sold and a price for goods established

2. The amount of goods available in the market to be sold at a given price

3. A person who performs real estate activities while employed by or associated with a broker

4. A person who acts as an intermediary on behalf of others for a fee or commission

5. The bringing together of parties interested in making a real estate transaction

6. The amount of goods people are willing and able to buy at a given price

_____broker

_____brokerage

_____demand

_____market

_____salesperson

_____supply

True and False

_____1. The five classes of real estate mentioned in the main text are residential, commercial, rental, agricultural and special-purpose.

_____2. A real estate broker's compensation may be in the form of a flat fee, hourly rate or a percentage of the amount of the transaction.

_____3. The supply of labor and the cost of construction generally have a direct effect on the demand for real estate in a market.

_____4. Population and demographics are two factors that tend to affect demand in the real estate market.

_____5. Warehouses, factories and power plants are examples of commercial property.

_____6. Members of the National Association of Real Estate Brokers are known as REALTORS®.

WRITE YOUR CORRECTIONS BELOW:

_____

_____

_____

_____

_____

_____

_____

_____

_____

_____

_____

Multiple Choice

1. Office buildings for sale and retail space for lease are examples of:

   a. commercial real estate
   b. special-use real estate.
   c. types of real property.
   d. properties that involve a tenant-landlord relationship.

2. In general, when the supply of a certain commodity decreases while demand remains the same, the price of that commodity will do which of the following?

   a. Tend to remain the same
   b. Tend to increase
   c. Decrease
   d. Price will not be affected.

3. All of the following factors will tend to affect demand *EXCEPT:*

   a. labor costs.
   b. employment levels.
   c. wage rates.
   d. demographics.

4. The population of a town suddenly increases. Which of the following is most likely to occur?

   a. Rental rates fall due to increased competition.
   b. Demand for housing decreases.
   c. Construction of new homes will be delayed.
   d. Real estate prices will increase.

5. Property management, appraisal, financing and development are all:

   a. specializations directly linked to state and federal government financial policies.
   b. separate professions within the real estate industry.
   c. real estate brokerage professions.
   d. demographic factors that affect demand for real property in a commercial market.

Illustration
Complete the illustration below by writing SUPPLY, DEMAND or PRICE on the arrows to illustrate the relationship among those factors.

Figure 1.1   **Effect of Supply and Demand on Price**

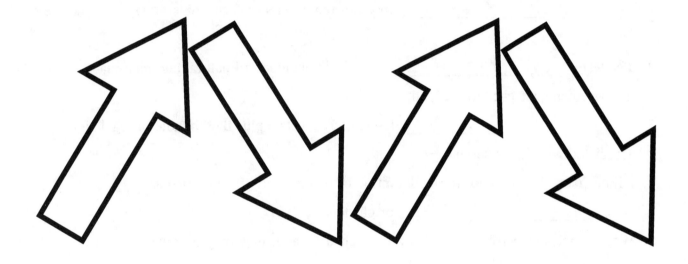

2 Real Property and the Law

Chapter Summary

1. _____ includes the earth's surface, mineral deposits and the air.

2. The term "_____" includes all natural and man-made improvements attached to the land.

3. _____ describes real estate plus the "bundle of legal rights" associated with its ownership.

4. All property that does not fit the definition of real property is classified as _____, or chattels.

5. When articles of personal property are attached to land, they may become _____, and are then considered a part of the real estate.

6. Personal property that is attached to real estate by a tenant for business purposes is classified as a _____ fixture and remains personal property.

7. Scarcity, improvements, permanence of investment and area preferences are the _____ characteristics of land.

8. Immobility, indestructibility and uniqueness are land's _____ characteristics.

9. A purchaser of real property actually purchases a _____ of legal rights to use the land in certain ways.

10. Every state and Canadian province has some type of _____ requirement for real estate brokers and salespeople.

Key Term Matching

1. An article installed by a tenant under a commercial lease, removable before the lease expires	_____accession
2. Any property that is not real property	_____air rights
3. Acquiring title to real property as a result of annexation or accretion	_____bundle of legal rights
4. Ownership of all legal rights to the land: control, possession, exclusion, enjoyment and disposition	_____fixture
5. The interests, benefits and rights of owning real estate	_____improvement
6. The right to use the open space above the surface of a property	_____personal property
7. A portion of the earth's surface extending down to the center and up into space, including all natural and artificial attachments	_____real estate
8. Ownership rights in the water, minerals, gas and oil that lie beneath a parcel of land	_____real property
9. Personal property that is converted to real property by being permanently attached to the realty	_____severance
10. Any structure or modification erected or imposed on a site to enhance the value of the property	_____subsurface rights
11. Changing an item of real estate to personal property by detaching it from the land	_____surface rights
12. Ownership rights excluding air or mineral rights accession	_____trade fixture

True and False

_____ 1. The terms "land," "real estate" and "real property" are interchangeable: they all refer to the same thing.

_____ 2. "Real property" is defined as the earth's surface extending downward to the center of the earth and upward to infinity, including permanent natural objects such as trees and water.

_____ 3. The term "real property" includes both land and real estate.

_____ 4. The transfer of the right to use the surface of the earth always includes the right to the natural resources that lie beneath the surface of the earth.

_____ 5. Trees, perennial shrubbery and grasses that do not require annual cultivation are considered personal property.

_____ 6. The process by which personal property becomes real property is referred to as "annexation."

_____ 7. A trade fixture is an article owned by a tenant and attached to a rented space or building used in conducting a business.

_____ 8. The economic characteristics of real estate are scarcity, improvements, permanence of investment and uniqueness.

_____ 9. Immobility, indestructibility and scarcity are physical characteristics of real property.

_____ 10. The image of a bundle of sticks is the traditional illustration of the set of legal rights of ownership.

WRITE YOUR CORRECTIONS BELOW:

_____

_____

_____

_____

_____

_____

_____

_____

_____

_____

_____

_____

Multiple Choice

1. Land and mineral rights in the land is the definition of:

   a. real property.   c. subsurface rights.
   b. real estate.   d. improvements.

2. *P* is the owner of Blueacre. *P* sells the rights to any gold lying beneath Blueacre to *GHI* Mining. *P* then sells the oil and gas rights to *JKL* Refineries. An existing chive farm on the property is sold to *MNO* Agribusiness. If a large deposit of uranium is discovered under Blueacre, it will be owned by:

   a. *GHI*.   c. *MNO*.
   b. *JKL*.   d. *P*.

3. Another word for *uniqueness* is:

   a. scarcity.
   b. nonhomogeneity.
   c. fructus industriales.
   d. immobility.

4. The bundle of legal rights includes all of the following *EXCEPT*:

   a. possession   c. exclusion
   b. control   d. expansion

5. Intent, method of annexation, adaptation and agreement are the legal tests for determining whether an item is:

   a. a chattel or an emblement.
   b. real property or personal property.
   c. land or real estate.
   d. fructus naturales or industriales.

6. Growing trees, fences and buildings would all be considered which of the following?

   a. Chattels   c. Fixtures
   b. Land   d. Real estate

7. *B* was looking for a new home. *B* particularly liked the ornate brass lighting fixtures in *H*'s house, and immediately made an offer, which *H* accepted. On moving day, *B* stormed into the real estate broker's office and demanded a refund: *H* had replaced all the ornate brass fixtures with plain steel ones. Which of the following, if true, would be *H*'s best defense?

   a. "Lighting fixtures are normally considered to be real estate."
   b. "The sales contract specifically excluded the lighting fixtures."
   c. "The lighting fixtures were personal property when I bought them at the store, so they're personal property forever."
   d. "The lighting fixtures belong to me because I installed them."

8. The most important economic characteristic of land is:

   a. permanence.
   b. area preference.
   c. uniqueness.
   d. possession.

Illustrations

Complete Figure 2.1 by identifying the five basic ownership rights in the blanks. Then label each of the sticks in the bundle as one of the rights. In Figure 2.2, use the checklist to characterize each item as real or personal property, and as a fixture or a trade fixture.

Figure 2.1   **The Bundle of Legal Rights**

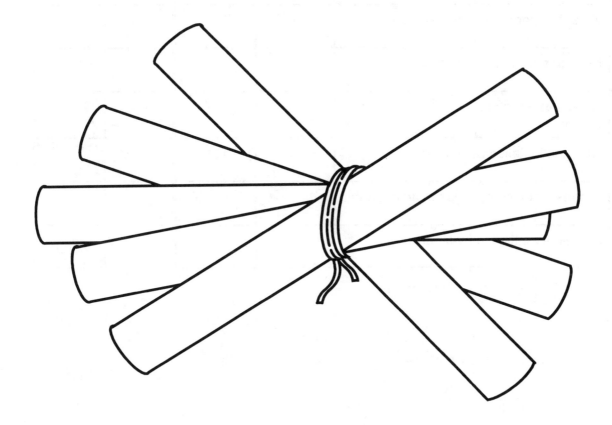

Figure 2.2   Real Property or Personal Property?

		Real Property	Personal Property	Fixture	Trade Fixture
1	Sidewalks and sewers in a subdivision				
2	Bushes surrounding a residence				
3	Wheat or corn crops on a farm				
4	Kitchen sink installed in a home				
5	Booths in a restaurant installed by a tenant				
6	Curtains installed by a tenant				
7	Pumps installed by a gas station tenant				
8	Machinery installed by landowner				

KEY
185

3 Concepts of Home Ownership

Chapter Summary

1. In a cooperative, owners receive a _____ as evidence of their right to occupy the unit in which they have an ownership interest.

2. One of the income tax benefits available to homeowners is the ability to _____ mortgage interest payments (with certain limitations) and property taxes from their federal income tax returns.

3. Income tax on the gain from a sale may be _____ if the homeowner buys and occupies a home of the same or similar value within 24 months.

4. Homeowners aged _____ or older are entitled to a one-time tax exclusion of up to $_____ of the gain from the sale of their home.

5. To protect their investment, most homeowners purchase _____.

6. _____ is factories, warehouses, office buildings or other structures that have been made suitable for residential use.

7. _____ homes are preassembled at a factory, trucked to the site and assembled on a foundation in less time that conventionally-built homes.

8. The four basic costs of home ownership are _____, _____, _____ and _____.

9. Many homeowners' policies contain a _____ clause that requires the policyholder to maintain insurance in an amount equal to _____ percent of the replacement cost of the home.

10. Homeowners in designated flood areas must obtain flood insurance to qualify for _____ mortgage loans.

Key Term Matching

1. A group of low-rise or high-rise rental residences that may include a number of amenities

2. A multiunit residential building owned by a corporation or trust and operated on behalf of stockholder/tenants who hold proprietary leases

3. A package policy against loss due to fire, theft and liability

4. Profit earned from the sale of an asset

5. A multiunit residential building in which tenants own their individual units in fee simple, plus an undivided joint interest in the common elements

6. A merging of diverse land uses into a self-contained community

7. The interest or value an owner has in property over and above any indebtedness

8. A clause in an insurance policy that requires the property to be insured at 80 percent of its replacement cost

9. A homeowner's interest in a property, as expressed by the property's purchase price, closing costs and improvements

10. A high-rise development that combines commercial and residential uses in a single structure

_____adjusted basis

_____apartment complex

_____capital gain

_____coinsurance

_____condominium

_____cooperative

_____equity

_____mixed-use development

_____planned unit development

_____standard home-owner's insurance

True and False

_____ 1. A cooperative is a form of residential ownership in which residents share ownership of common areas while owning their own units individually.

_____ 2. Warehouses, factories, office buildings, hotels and other structures that have been converted to residential use are referred to as planned unit developments.

_____ 3. Under the traditional rule of thumb used by lenders to determine whether a prospective buyer can afford a home, PITI should not exceed 28 percent of monthly income, and payment on all debts should not exceed 36 percent of gross monthly income.

_____ 4. Under the rule of thumb traditionally used by lenders to determine whether or not a prospective buyer can afford a home, expenses such as insurance premiums, utilities and routine medical care are considered to be covered by a buyer's excess monthly income.

_____ 5. Equity represents the "paid off" share of a property, held free of any mortgage.

_____ 6. Capital gain is the profit realized from the sale or exchange of an asset.

_____ 7. Taxpayers over the age of 55 are entitled to a one-time deferment of taxation of up to $125,000 of the gain from the sale or exchange of their principal residence.

_____ 8. A part of the profit on the sale of a principal residence is exempt from immediate taxation if a similar residence of the same or greater value is bought and occupied within 24 months of the sale.

_____ 9. Under standard homeowner's insurance policies, the insured is usually required to maintain insurance equal to at least 41 percent of the replacement cost of the dwelling, including the price of the land.

_____ 10. If a borrower's property is located in a designated flood area, there are no exemptions from the flood insurance requirement under the National Flood Insurance Act.

WRITE YOUR CORRECTIONS BELOW:

_____

_____

_____

_____

_____

_____

_____

_____

_____

_____

_____

_____

Multiple Choice

1. *Equity* refers to the:

   a. profit realized from the sale or exchange of real property.
   b. total amount of prinicpal and interest plus tax and insurance.
   c. difference between the amount owed on a mortgage and the property's market value.
   d. amount of gain that may be deferred for income tax purposes.

2. Which type of residence, depending on state law, may be considered either real or personal property?

   a. Converted-use properties.
   b. Condominiums.
   c. High-rise residential units.
   d. Mobile homes.

3. Why does it matter whether the form of home in the previous question is classified as real or personal property?

   a. Real estate licensees may not be permitted to sell personal property.
   b. Personal property usually costs less than real property.
   c. There are tax advantages to owning personal property.
   d. The difference is strictly a matter of legal theory, with no practical use.

4. *K*'s homeowner's insurance policy contains a coinsurance provision. If *K*'s home is damaged by a covered event, which of the following statements is true?

   a. *K*'s claim will be settled for the actual cash value of the damage.
   b. *K*'s claim will be prorated by dividing the percentage of replacement cost by the minimum coverage requirement.
   c. *K* may make a claim for the full cost of the repair without deduction for depreciation.
   d. *K* may make a claim for the depreciated value of the damage.

5. *T* was born at 554 Peachtree Street in 1927, and lived there until 1992, when *T* sold the house to *M*. In 1993, *T* bought 554 Peachtree back from *M* and lived there until 1997, when *T* sold the house and moved to an apartment in another state. Is *T* entitled to the over-55 exclusion on this transaction?

   a. Yes, because *T* owned the house for at least three of the last five years prior to the sale.
   b. No, because *T* has not owned the house as a principal residence for at least five years prior to the sale.
   c. Yes, because *T* lived in the house for at least 55 years prior to sale.
   d. No, because *T* did not purchase a residence of equal or greater value within 24 months of the sale.

6. A development that includes office space, stores and residential units could be an example of any of the following *EXCEPT* a:

   a. converted use property.
   b. mixed-use development.
   c. planned unit development.
   d. condominium property.

7. *R* was born on July 10, 1944. *R* has lived in the same house for 5 years. When *R* sells the house on July 12, 1997, any gain from the sale of the home may:

   a. be taxed at a lower rate because of *R*'s age.
   b. not be deferred, because *R* has lived in the house for fewer than 8 years.
   c. deferred if another house of equal or greater value is purchased within 24 months.
   d. be excluded from income taxation up to $125,000 because of *R*'s age and time-in-residence.

8. *T*'s house is 450 feet outside a designated flood-prone area. If *T* applies for a federally-related mortgage loan, *T*'s mortgage lender:

   a. may require flood insurance.
   b. must require flood insurance.
   c. is prohibited by federal law from requiring flood insurance.
   d. may invoke the National Flood Insurance Act for properties lying inside, or within 500 feet of, a designated flood-prone area.

9. *B*, a prospective buyer, wants to purchase a house. The mortgage payment (principal and interest) will be $1,750. The monthly insurance and tax impounds will be $70. The buyer's other recurring monthly debts total $2,925. If *B*'s gross monthly income is $6,500, will *B* qualify for a loan if the lender uses a strict rule-of-thumb method?

   a. No, because the PITI exceeds 28 percent of *B*'s gross monthly income.
   b. Yes, because the PITI is less than 41 percent of *B*'s gross monthly income.
   c. No, because *B*'s other debts exceed 36 percent of *B*'s gross monthly income.
   d. Yes, because *B*'s other debts exceed 28 percent of *B*'s gross monthly income.

10. All of the expenses may be deducted from a homeowner's gross income for income tax purposes *EXCEPT*:

   a. loan repayment penalties.
   b. loan discount points.
   c. interest paid on overdue real estate taxes.
   d. real estate taxes.

11. In the past 42 months, *T* has made regular rental payments on Creaking Cottage. *T*'s rent is $865 per month. The property owner, *O*, purchased Creaking Cottage as an investment four years ago for $125,000. The property's value has already appreciated to $150,000. *O* still owes $65,000 on a mortgage loan used to finance the purchase of the house. Based on these facts, what is *T*'s current equity in Creaking Cottage?

    a. $0
    b. $36,330
    c. $60,000
    d. $88,670

Illustration

A real estate broker keeps a scrapbook of newspaper advertisements, organized by housing type, for various properties on the coffee table in the conference room. Figure 3.1 illustrates the most recent ads. Update the broker's scrapbook by identifying the type of housing described in each advertisement.

Figure 3.1   Forms of Ownership

HERE'S A TIP: BUY STOCK IN YOUR HOME! Select units are now available in Gleason Tower: Lavish 4- and 5-bedroom apartments with all the extras! Approved buyers become stockholders in Gleason Tower Corp. From $97,000

Live where you work:
Logan Village
This quiet, tree-lined new community features lots of open space. Shops, schools and recreation: Logan Village has it all! Townhomes start mid80's; residences from $125,000

CLOCK TOWER LOFTS
The old Mennsen-Hart Watch Factory is now 20 fabulous luxury lofts above the exclusive **Watchmaker's Mall**! Studios, 1&2 bd; security. From $1,200/month

THE SKY'S YOUR LIMIT...
DOWNTOWN'S TALLEST BUILDING OFFERS STUNNING VIEWS, SUPER AMENITIES, FIVE WORLD-CLASS RESTAURANTS, GREAT SHOPPING AND LIFESTYLE SERVICES ALL UNDER ONE 85TH FLOOR ROOFTOP GARDEN!
RESIDENCES START ON 62. FROM THE MID-500s

```
1275 Oak View Terrace
3 bdrm, 2 ba unit; dining
rm, pool, 24-hr doorman.
$110,500; monthly asmt
only $475
```

Arboure Valie Club
2 bedroom/2bath unit with balcony. Utilities paid; no pets. Pool, tennis, golf. Private forest preserve. $1,200/mo; avail. 5/1

4 Agency

Chapter Summary

1. The law of _____ governs the principal-agent relationship.

2. Agency relationships may be expressed by the words of the parties, by express written agreement or _____ by their actions.

3. In _____-agency relationships the broker/agent represents one party, either the buyer or the seller, in the transaction.

4. If an agent elicits the assistance of other brokers who cooperate in the transaction, the other brokers may become _____ of the principal.

5. Many states have adopted statutes that replace the _____ law of agency and that establish the responsibilities and duties of the parties.

6. A _____ acts as an intermediary between a buyer and seller, but represents neither party.

7. Representing two opposing parties in the same transaction is referred to as _____.

8. The source of compensation for the client services _____ determine the party who is being represented.

9. Licensees have certain duties and obligations to both clients and _____.

10. Consumers are entitled to _____ dealing and the information

    necessary for them to make informed decisions.

Key Term Matching, Part I

1. The basic framework that governs the legal responsibilities of an agent to a principal

2. An agent who is authorized to represent the principal in one specific act or business transaction, under detailed instructions

3. The individual who is authorized and consents to represent the interests of another person

4. The establishment of an agency relationship as the result of the actions of the parties

5. The individual who hires and delegates to the agent the responsibility of representing his or her interests

6. The fiduciary relationship between the principal and the agent

7. Nonfraudulent exaggeration of a property's benefits or features

8. An agent authorized to represent the principal in a broad range of matters related to a specific business or activity

9. In a real estate agency relationship, the third party who is entitled to honesty and fair dealing

10. An intermediary between a buyer and seller who assists both parties with a transaction, but who represents neither party

_____ agency

_____ agent

_____ customer

_____ general agent

_____ implied agreement

_____ law of agency

_____ nonagent

_____ principal

_____ puffing

_____ special agent

Key Term Matching, Part II

1. An agency relationship in which the agent represents two principals simultaneously, without their knowledge or permission

2. A contract in which the parties formally state their intention to establish an agency relationship

3. Real estate licensees who represent buyers exclusively

4. An agent empowered to do anything the principal could do personally

5. A property that has been branded as undesirable because of the events that occurred in or near it

6. The principal in a real estate agency relationship

7. An agency relationship in which the agent represents two principals simultaneously, with their knowledge or permission

8. Care, obedience, accounting, loyalty and disclosure

9. The party to whom an agent delegates some of his or her authority

10. A hidden structural problem that would not be discovered by ordinary inspection

_____ buyer's brokers

_____ client

_____ common-law duties

_____ disclosed dual agency

_____ express agreement

_____ latent defect

_____ stigmatized property

_____ subagent

_____ undisclosed dual agency

_____ universal agent

True and False

_____ 1. The individual who hires and delegates to the agent the responsibility of representing his or her other interests is the fiduciary.

_____ 2. Facilitators, transaction brokers, transaction coordinators and contract brokers are all examples of nonagents.

_____ 3. An agent works with the client and for the customer.

_____ 4. Under the common law of agency, the agent owes his or her principal the five duties of care, obedience, accounting, loyalty and disclosure.

_____ 5. The common law fiduciary duty of obedience obligates the agent to act in good faith at all times and obey all the principal's instructions.

_____ 6. The common law duty of loyalty requires that an agent not disclose the principal's financial situation or facts about the condition of the property.

_____ 7. Implied agency relationships are generally illegal unless the agent receives the informed, written consent of all parties.

_____ 8. The source of compensation is the key determining factor in whether or not an agency relationship exists.

_____ 9. A general agent is empowered to do anything the principal could do personally, with virtually no limitation on his or her authority to act.

_____ 10. A real estate broker is usually the general agent of a buyer or seller.

_____ 11. The only difference between a buyer's agent and a seller's agent is that a buyer's agent owes the principal different fiduciary duties.

_____ 12. In a dual agency relationship, the agent represents two principals in the same transaction.

_____ 13. A dual agency relationship is legal if either the buyer or the seller consents to the dual representation.

_____ 14. An agent owes a client the duties of reasonable care and skill, honest and fair dealing, and disclosure of known facts.

_____ 15. A negligent misrepresentation occurs when the broker engages in exaggeration of a property's benefits or features.

_____ 16. When a property has a hidden structural defect that could not be discovered by ordinary inspection, it is referred to as a stigmatized property.

WRITE YOUR CORRECTIONS BELOW:

_____

_____

_____

_____

_____

_____

_____

_____

_____

_____

_____

_____

_____

Multiple Choice

1. An individual who is authorized and consents to represent the interests of another person is a/an:

    a. client.
    c. agent.
    b. principal.
    d. facilitator.

2. Broker *N* represents *C*, but is currently working with *K* to find a home. Assuming that no statute has replaced the traditional common law, which of the following correctly identifies the parties in this relationship?

    a. *N* is *K*'s agent; *C* is *N*'s client.
    b. *K* is *N*'s client; *C* is *N*'s principal.
    c. *C* is *N*'s customer; *K* is *N*'s client.
    d. *N* is *C*'s agent; *K* is *N*'s customer.

3. The agent's obligation to use his or her skill and expertise on behalf of the principal arises under which of the common-law duties?

    a. Care
    c. Loyalty
    b. Obedience
    d. Disclosure

4. An agent representing the seller has a duty to disclose all of the following to his or her principal *EXCEPT:*

    a. ridiculously low offers.
    b. the buyer's financial ability to offer a higher price.
    c. the agent's advertising budget.
    d. the buyer's intention to resell the property for a profit.

5. *J*, a broker, has an agency agreement to represent the seller, *M*, in the sale of Grandview Mansion. The agreement's expiration date is June 10. On May 5, Grandview Mansion is struck by lightning and burns to the ground. *M*, overwhelmed by grief, dies. Based on these facts, which of the following is true?

    a. The agency agreement was terminated by the fire, although *M*'s death also would have done so.
    b. The agency agreement was not terminated until *M*'s death on June 11.
    c. If Grandview Mansion had not been destroyed by the fire, *M*'s death would not have terminated the agreement: J would become the broker for *M*'s estate.
    d. Only the mutual agreement of the parties can terminate a valid agency agreement before its expiration date.

6. A person who is designated by the principal in a broad range of matters related to a particular transaction or activity is a/an:

    a. universal agent.
    b. special agent.
    c. designated agent.
    d. general agent.

7. Z, a real estate broker, signed an agency agreement with a seller, V. The asking price for V's house was $98,500. A few days later, Z met Q at a charity dinner. Q was interested in buying a home in the $95,000 to $110,000 price range. Z agreed to help Q locate such a property and to represent Q in negotiating a favorable purchase price.

Based on these facts, which of the following statements is true?

a. Z's relationships with Q and V are separate issues, and no dual agency question arises.
b. V is Z's client, and Q is Z's customer; there is no dual agency problem.
c. Z has created a potential undisclosed dual agency problem, and should disclose the relationships to both parties before showing V's home to Q.
d. Z has created a dual agency problem, and should immediately terminate the agreement with either V or Q.

8. Broker T is showing a house to a prospective buyer. T points out the "rustic charm" of the sagging front porch and refers to a weed-choked backyard as a "delightful garden." T is engaging in which of the following?

a. Intentional misrepresentation
b. Negligent misrepresentations
c. Puffing
d. Fraud

9. A house built over a ditch covered with decaying timber, or ceilings that are improperly attached to the support beams are examples of:

a. stigmatized properties.
b. environmental hazards.
c. latent defects.
d. conditions that need not be disclosed.

10. The agent and the principal entered into a written agency agreement. The agent was authorized to represent the principal in a single transaction. Later, the buyer and seller agreed that the buyer would pay the agent's commission. On the basis of these facts, all of the following may be assumed EXCEPT:

a. the principal and the agent had an express agency agreement.
b. the agency agreement in this transaction established a special agency.
c. the agent represented the buyer.
d. the agent represented the principal.

Illustrations

In Figures 4.1 through 4.4, the squares represent agents and the circles represent clients or customers. For each figure, illustrate the appropriate agency relationship by connecting the appropriate circles and squares. Label each one "AGENT," "CLIENT" "CUSTOMER," "BUYER" and "SELLER" as necessary. <u>Illustrate only one relationship in each figure</u> (you may have blank circles or squares left over). In Figure 4.5, find the five traditional fiduciary duties of an agent in the Word-Finder Puzzle. The words may be spelled backward or forward, and may not be in a straight line.

Figure 4.1   **Single Agency (Seller's Agent)**

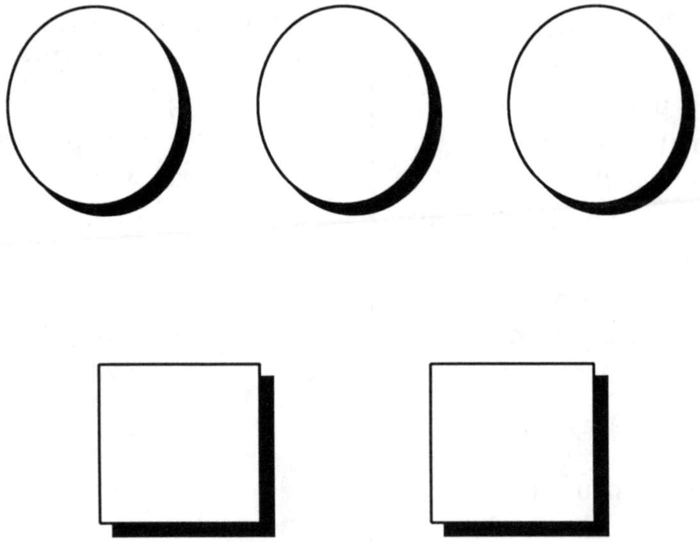

Figure 4.2   Dual Agency

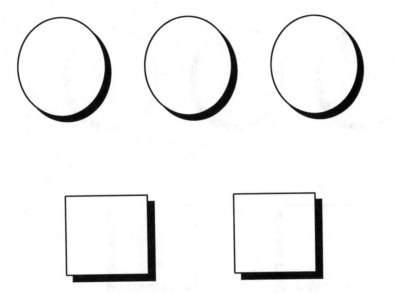

Figure 4.3   Subagency

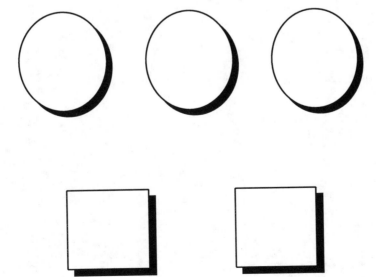

Figure 4.4   **Single Agency (Buyer's Agent)**

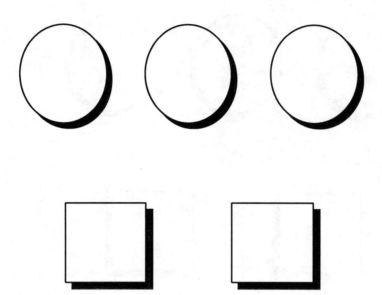

Figure 4.5 The Five Common-Law Fiduciary Duties of an Agent

```
R  E  W  A  E  V  H  D  T  L  O  B
A  S  Y  R  V  S  Q  B  M  O  P  L
C  O  A  L  Y  B  C  A  R  B  O  V
C  A  L  O  Y  S  V  B  M  E  A  C
Y  L  O  Y  A  L  T  Y  L  D  Y  C
C  K  L  A  Y  A  C  C  O  I  U  E
N  T  I  N  G  D  I  S  C  E  U  R
D  O  Y  A  L  T  Y  A  C  N  N  U
A  G  N  I  T  N  U  O  C  C  A  S
T  Y  B  E  D  E  I  N  A  E  B  O
B  E  N  C  E  A  C  O  U  I  E  L
A  C  O  N  T  E  L  Y  T  A  L  C
B  C  H  H  A  L  D  L  O  D  I  S
```

KEY 189

5 | Real Estate Brokerage

Chapter Summary

1. _____ govern the professional conduct of brokers and salespeople.

2. State license laws are enacted to _____ by ensuring a standard of competence and professionalism in the real estate industry.

3. _____ is the act of bringing people together, for a fee or commission, who wish to buy, sell, exchange or lease real estate.

4. The broker's compensation in a real estate sale may take the form of a flat fee, hourly rate or_____.

5. The listing broker is considered to have earned a commission when he or she procures a _____, _____ and _____ buyer for a seller.

6. The _____ works on the broker's behalf as either an employee or an independent contractor.

7. Federal and state _____ laws prohibit brokers from conspiring to fix prices, engage in boycotts, allocate customers or markets, or establish tie-in agreements.

Key Term Matching

1. The common law doctrine of "let the buyer beware"

2. Statutes enacted by state legislatures to protect the public and ensure a standard of competence in the real estate industry

3. The device by which a state licensing authority defines and enforces the statutory law

4. The business of bringing parties together

5. An individual who is licensed to buy, sell, exchange or lease property for others, and to charge a fee for those services

6. A company held by a single owner

7. A person who is licensed only to perform real estate activities on behalf of a broker

8. A salesperson whose activities are closely controlled, and who is entitled to benefits, unemployment compensation and income tax withholding

9. A licensee who works under the terms of a written contract and receives more than 90 percent of his or her income from sales production rather than hours worked

10. A form of compensation computed as a percentage of the total sales price of a property

11. The broker who starts a chain of events that results in the sale of a property

12. A person who is prepared to buy on the seller's terms

13. A conspiracy by two or more businesses against another

14. An illegal division of territories to avoid competition

_____ allocation of markets

_____ brokerage

_____ caveat emptor

_____ commission

_____ employee

_____ group boycotting

_____ independent contractor

_____ procuring cause

_____ ready, willing and able buyer

_____ real estate broker

_____ real estate license laws

_____ rules and regulations

_____ salesperson

_____ sole proprietorship

True and False

_____ 1. Most of the states regulate the activities of real estate brokers and salespeople.

_____ 2. The purpose of the real estate license laws is to regulate the real estate industry and protect the constitutional rights of property owners.

_____ 3. A real estate salesperson is licensed to buy, sell, exchange or lease real property for others, and to charge a fee for those services.

_____ 4. A real estate agent is an individual who is licensed to perform real estate activities on behalf of a licensed broker.

_____ 5. The Internal Revenue Service has established criteria for determining whether a real estate licensee is classified as an employee or an independent contractor for income tax purposes.

_____ 6. The amount of a broker's compensation is always negotiable.

_____ 7. A broker is considered to be the procuring cause of a sale if he or she is present at the time the transaction closes.

_____ 8. Price-fixing, group boycotting and allocation of markets are three examples of antitrust violations.

_____ 9. The practice of setting standard prices for products or services is referred to as a tie-in arrangement.

_____10. In a civil suit based on an antitrust violation by a real estate licensee, the injured party may recover three times the value of actual damages.

WRITE YOUR CORRECTIONS BELOW:

_____

_____

_____

_____

_____

_____

_____

_____

_____

_____

_____

_____

Multiple Choice

1. Real estate license laws have been enacted in all fifty states. The purpose of these laws is to:

   a. protect licensees from lawsuits.
   b. protect the public and establish standards of professionalism.
   c. protect the public and prevent licensees from engaging in profit-making activities.
   d. establish maximum levels of competency and a moral marketplace.

2. A real estate salesperson is:

   a. an independent contractor.
   b. an employee of a licensed broker.
   c. a licensee who performs real estate activities on behalf of a broker.
   d. a combination office manager, markter and organizer with a fundamental understanding of the real estate industry, who may or may not be licensed.

3. All of the following are the indicators of independent contractor status used by the Internal Revenue Service, *EXCEPT*:

    a. a current real estate license.
    b. specific hours stated in a written agreement.
    c. a written agreement that specifies that the individual will not be treated as an employee for tax purposes.
    d. 90 percent or more of the individual's income is based on sales production rather than hours worked.

4. *J*, a broker, owns Happy Homes Realty. None of the salespeople employed by *J* is permitted to charge less than an 8 percent commission in any transaction. *F*, also a broker, owns Open Door Homefinders. After reading a newspaper article about *J*'s policy, *F* decides to adopt the 8 percent minimum, too. Based on these facts, which of the following statements is true?

    a. *J*'s policy is price fixing, and violates the antitrust law.
    b. Although *J*'s original policy was legal, *F*'s adoption of the minimum commission may constitute an antitrust violation if *J* and *F* are in the same real estate market.
    c. Both *F* and *J* have engaged in illegal price fixing.
    d. Neither *F* nor *J* has committed an antitrust violation.

5. *N*, a real estate broker, had a listing agreement with *S*, a seller. Under the agreement, *N* was entitled to a 6 percent commission. *N* showed *S*'s home to *B*, a prospective buyer. The next day, *B* called *S* and offered to buy the house for 5 percent less than the asking price. *S* agreed to the sale, and informed *N* in writing that no further brokerage services would be required. The sale went to closing six weeks later. Based on these facts, which of the following statements is true?

    a. While *N* was the procuring cause of the sale, *S* properly canceled the contract; without a valid employment agreement in force at the time of closing, *N* is not entitled to a commission.
    b. *N* is entitled to a partial commission, and *B* is obligated to pay it.
    c. Under the facts as stated, *N* is not the procuring cause of this sale but is still entitled to a commission.
    d. *N* was the procuring cause of this sale, and is entitled to the full 6 percent commission.

6. A qualified buyer makes a written offer on a property on March 6 by filling out and signing a sales agreement. Later that day, the seller accepts and signs the agreement. The broker gives a copy of the signed agreement to the buyer on March 8, and to the seller on March 11. The seller's deed is delivered on May 1. The deed is recorded on May 7, and the buyer takes possession on May 15. On which date is the broker's commission earned if the listing agreement, the sales contract and state law are silent on the issue?

   a. March 6   c. March 11
   b. March 8   d. May 1

7. In Question 6, when is the broker's commission *payable* if this is a "usual" transaction?

   a. March 11   c. May 7
   b. May 1   d. May 15

8. At MNO Realty, salespeople pay a monthly "desk rent" based on 15 percent of their monthly income. In May, salesperson *G* receives 6 percent on a $95,000 sale, 7½ percent on a $105,250 sale and 6¾ percent on an $89,500 sale. The only other salesperson at MNO who received a commission in May got 7 percent on a $128,000 sale, how much did MNO receive in May?

   a. $4,289.25   c. $12,251.53
   b. $7,095.97   d. $14,945.00

9. All of the following are violations of the federal antitrust laws, *EXCEPT:*

   a. group boycotting.
   b. allocation of customers.
   c. commission splitting.
   d. tying agreements.

10. Salespeople in PQR Realty are compensated based on the following formula: 35 percent of the commission earned on any sale, less a $150 per transaction desk rental. Salespeople are responsible for paying 75 percent of all marketing and sales expenses for any property they list, and a $50 per transaction fee to cover the monthly expenses of advertising and marketing PQR's services. If a salesperson sold a house for $128,000, with a 6 percent commission, how much would he or she be paid if the sale incurred $347.75 in marketing and advertising costs?

    a. $2,227.19   c. $2,545.62
    b. $2,246.09   d. $7,273.19

Illustrations

In Figure 5.1, read each statement and then write the name of the speaker in the appropriate box in Open Door Realty's organizational chart. In Figure 5.2, fill in the table of license requirements and fees based on your state's license laws, rules and regulations.

Figure 5.1   **Open Door Realty's Organizational Chart**

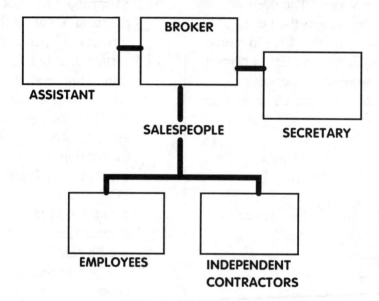

Tim: "I am a licensed real estate salesperson. I earn half my income from an hourly salary, and half from sales."

Ron: "I have a real estate license, but my job is limited to marketing and office management activities."

Bob: "I am a real estate licensee. I work under a contract with the broker, and earn all of my income from sales."

Joyce: "I'm a licensed real estate salesperson. I set my own hours and pay my own income taxes."

Elaine: "I'm licensed to buy, sell, exchange or lease real property for a fee."

Sandra: "I am licensed to perform real estate activities on behalf of a broker. I have health insurance and a retirement plan."

Dora: "Although I don't have a real estate license, I work closely with the licensees to ensure that the office runs smoothly and transactions go to closing."

Figure 5.2   State License Requirements and Fees

LICENSE REQUIREMENTS	SALESPERSON	BROKER
Age		
Education		
Experience		
Bond		
Recommendations		
Photograph		
Fingerprints		
Continuing education		
Licensure period		
Expiration date		
FEES	SALESPERSON	BROKER
Application	$	$
Registration for examination	$	$
Phone or fax registration	$	$
Examination	$	$
Recovery fund	$	$
Concurrent license	$	$
Renewals	$	$
License by reciprocity	$	$
Corporations	$	$
Branch office	$	$
Transfer	$	$
Activation of inactive license	$	$
Reinstatement	$	$
Bad check penalty	$	$
Other	$	$

6 Listing Agreements and Buyer Representation

Chapter Summary

1. A listing agreement is an _____, rather than a real estate contract.

2. A listing agreement creates a _____ agency relationship between the principal (the owner of the property) and the agent (the broker).

3. In an _____ listing, one broker is appointed as the seller's sole agent, and is given the exclusive right to market the property.

4. In an _____ listing, one broker is authorized to act as the principal's sole agent; however, the seller retains the right to market the property independently, and is not obligated to pay the broker a commission if the seller finds a buyer.

5. In an _____ listing, the seller retains the right to employ any number of brokers as agents, and is obligated to pay a commission only to the one who successfully locates a buyer.

6. A _____ is a marketing organization whose broker members make their own exclusive listings available through other brokers.

7. Because of the potential for a conflict of interest between a broker's fiduciary responsibility to the seller and the broker's profit motive, _____ listings are illegal in many states and discouraged in others.

8. An _____ listing gives the broker the right to purchase the listed property.

9. All listing agreements should specify a definite _____ date.

10. A salesperson or broker can help the seller determine a listing price for the property by preparing a _____, a comparison of the prices of properties recently sold, those currently on the market and those properties that did not sell.

11. _____ is the most probable price property would bring in an arm's-length transaction under normal conditions on the open market.

12. Like a listing agreement, a _____ is also an employment contract, in which the broker is employed by a prospective purchaser.

13. In an _____ buyer agency agreement, the buyer is legally bound to compensate the agent whenever a suitable property is purchased, regardless of whether or not the agent located the property.

14. In an _____ buyer agency agreement, the broker is entitled to payment only if he or she locates the property that the buyer ultimately purchases.

15. A non-exclusive agency contract between a broker and a buyer, under which the buyer may enter into similar agreements with any number of brokers, is referred to as an _____ buyer agency agreement.

Key Term Matching

1. An employment contract for a broker's services

2. A listing agreement under which the seller must pay the broker a commission regardless of who sells the property

3. A listing agreement with a single broker, under which the seller retains the right to sell the property independently, without being obligated to pay a commission

4. A listing agreement in which the seller may employ multiple brokers, retains the right to market the property independently, and is obligated to compensate only the broker who produces a buyer, if any

5. A marketing organization whose broker members make their own exclusive listings available to other brokers

6. A listing agreement in which the seller receives a specific dollar amount from the sales price, and the selling broker retains the balance as his or her compensation

7. A listing agreement in which the broker has the right to purchase the listed property

8. A comparison of the sales prices of similar properties

9. A contract between a buyer and a buyer's broker that permits the buyer to enter into an unlimited number of similar agreements

10. A contract between a buyer and a buyer's broker in which the agent is entitled to compensation even if the buyer finds a suitable property independently

11. An agreement between a broker and a buyer in which the broker's right to payment is contingent on his or her locating the property ultimately purchased by the buyer

_____ CMA

_____ exclusive agency buyer listing

_____ exclusive-agency listing

_____ exclusive buyer agency

_____ exclusive-right-to-sell listing

_____ listing agreement

_____ MLS

_____ net listing

_____ open buyer agency

_____ open listing

_____ option listing

True and False

_____ 1. Under a typical net listing, the broker's commission is based on a percentage of the seller's net from the transaction.

_____ 2. A listing agreement is a contract for the sale of real estate.

_____ 3. The parties to a listing agreement are a broker or salesperson and a buyer or a seller.

_____ 4. The salesperson sets the listing price for a property by using a competitive market analysis.

_____ 5. A listing agreement in which the seller retains the right to employ any number of brokers as agent is referred to as a multiple listing.

_____ 6. In an exclusive-right-to-sell listing, one broker is authorized to act as the exclusive agent of the principal, who retains the right to sell the property without obligation to the broker.

_____ 7. In buyer agency, the source of compensation is the major factor that determines the relationship.

_____ 8. In an exclusive-right-to-seil listing, the seller must pay the broker's commission even if the seller finds a buyer without the broker's assistance.

_____ 9. In an exclusive buyer agency agreement, the broker is entitled to payment only if he or she locates the property that the buyer ultimately purchases.

_____ 10. A listing contract ordinarily creates an open listing unless it specifically states otherwise.

_____ 11. Because a listing agreement is a personal service contract between a broker and seller, the broker may transfer the listing to another broker with or without the seller's consent.

_____ 12. A listing agreement should not include such details as which items of personal property stay with the real estate, or the disposition of leased equipment.

_____

_____

_____

_____

_____

_____

_____

_____

_____

_____

_____

Multiple Choice

1. *L* wants to net $60,000 on the sale of Blackacre. *L*'s broker will charge a 7 percent commission. To obtain the desired net price, what must the gross selling price of Blackacre be (rounded to the nearest dollar)?

   a. $55,800   c. $63,830
   b. $60,000   d. $64,516

2. In a typical buyer agency agreement, the buyer is the:

   a. principal.
   b. customer.
   c. agent.
   d. employee.

3. Salesperson *F* is employed by Broker *Y*. It is *Y*'s office policy that salespeople keep 60 percent of the firm's share of any commission earned from any property they list. *F* listed a property that was later sold by Broker *X* for \$114,000. If the two brokers agree to split the 6.5 percent commission equally, what will *F* receive?

   a. \$2,223 c. \$3,705
   b. \$2,923 d. \$4,440

4. *G* listed her home for sale with Broker *K*. However, when *G* sold the home herself, she didn't owe anyone a commission. Based on these facts, what type of listing did *G* and *K* most likely sign?

   a. Exclusive-right-to-sell listing
   b. Net listing
   c. Multiple listing
   d. Open listing

5. The commission on the sale of 119 South Wright was \$10,875, based on a 7½ percent commission rate. What was the final selling price of 119 South Wright?

   a. \$81,563 c. \$117,560
   b. \$100,875 d. \$145,000

6. All of the following information is generally included in a listing agreement *EXCEPT:*

   a. the dimensions of the lot.
   b. the most recent year's property taxes.
   c. the client's specific requirements for a suitable property.
   d. agency and property condition disclosures.

7. Salesperson *H* is employed by broker *B*. On January 10, *H* met with a seller and described the advantages of listing the seller's property with broker *B*'s office. On January 15, the seller agreed to the listing: H and the seller signed the agreement. On January 18, *B* signed the listing agreement as required by office policy. On January 20, *H* posted a "For Sale" sign in front of the house. When did the listing agreement become effective?

   a. January 10 c. January 18
   b. January 15 d. January 20

8. *B* listed *D*'s home for \$111,250 under a 90-day exclusive-right-to-sell listing agreement with a 6 percent commission. The next week, *B* began advertising the home in a local paper and showed the property to two prospective buyers. Later that week, *D* announced that he had decided to sell his home to a relative for \$95,000. *D* is liable to *B* for:

   a. \$975. c. \$6,675.
   b. \$5,700. d. \$16,250

9. The listed price of a property is always:

   a. negotiable.
   b. a function of market value.
   c. the seller's decision.
   d. determined by a CMA.

10. Which of the following accurately expresses the formula for determining the actual percentage of the sales price paid to the broker?

   a. Price x (100% – Commission) = Rate
   b. Price ÷ Commission = Rate
   c. Price x Rate = Commission
   d. Commission ÷ Price = Rate

Illustration

Figures 6.1, 6.2 and 6.3 illustrate three types of listing contracts. The squares are sellers, the circles are brokers and the triangles are buyers, and the arrows illustrate relationships. Give each figure a title based on the type of contract it illustrates. Figure 6.4 is part of a listing worksheet. Fill it in, using John and Martha Rambler's property at 1232 Ida Lane, depicted on page 48. The scale is 1 inch = 12 feet. <u>Approximate dimensions are acceptable</u>. Assume central air, gas heat, brick siding and a shingle roof. The property is about twenty years old, and has no basement. You may make any other assumptions about the property's characteristics and features. There is no answer key for Figure 6.4, which is for practice only.

Figure 6.1   "  "

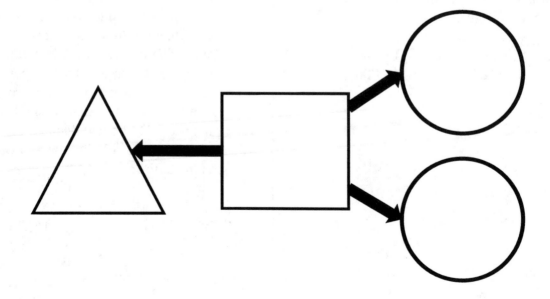

Figure 6.2

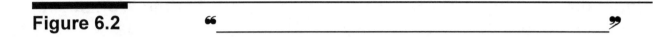

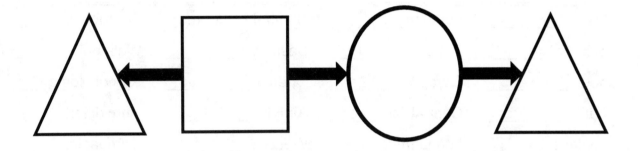

Figure 6.3

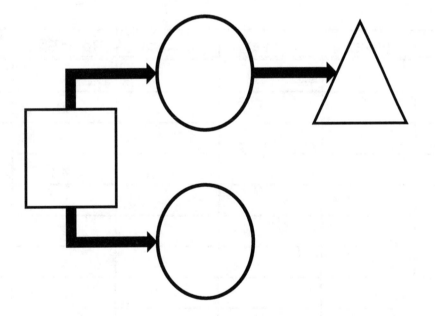

Figure 6.4   Listing Worksheet

Owners_____ Address _____

Reason for Selling_____

Style_____	Lot Size_____	Number of Rooms__	Bedrooms_____
Deck Size_____	Patio Size_____	Basement_____	Walk-out_____
Shed _____	Garage_____	Opener_____	Age of Home____
Heat_____	Central Air_____	Air Filter_____	Humidifier _____
Fireplace_____	Log Lighter_____	Wet Bar_____	Compactor_____
Range/Oven_____	Gas Grill_____	Dishwasher_____	Disposal_____
Siding_____	Story_____	Roof_____	Other_____
Water_____	Fence_____	Sewer_____	Other_____

ROOMS	LEVEL	CARPET	DRAPES	ROOM SIZE	COMMENTS
Living Room				x	
Dining Room				x	
Kitchen				x	
Family Room				x	
Rec. Room				x	
Bedroom				x	
Bedroom				x	
Bedroom				x	
Bedroom				x	
Bath: Full				x	
Bath: ¾				x	
Bath: ½				x	

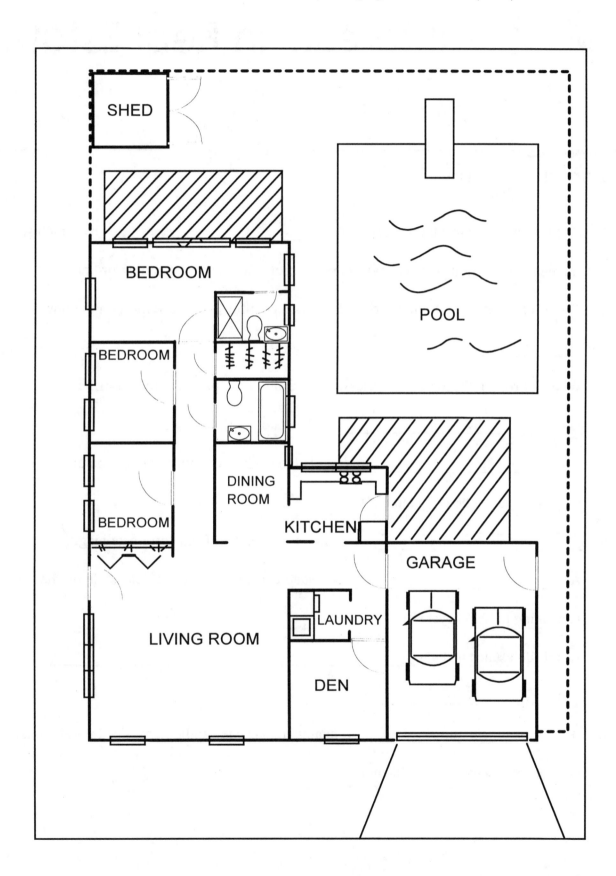

7   Interests in Real Estate

Chapter Summary

1. One of the government's powers is the _____, by which states can enact legislation such as environmental protection laws and zoning ordinances.

2. The government may acquire privately owned land for public use through the power of _____.

3. When a property becomes ownerless, ownership of the property may transfer, or _____, to the state.

4. An _____ is the degree, quantity, nature and extent of interest a person holds in land.

5. _____ estates are estates of indeterminate length.

6. A _____ estate can be absolute, or defeasible on the happening of some event.

7. Legal life estates include _____, _____ and _____.

8. _____ against real estate can be liens, deed restrictions, easements, licenses or encroachments.

9. An _____ is the right acquired by one person to use another's real estate.

10. _____ easements involve two separately owned tracts. The tract benefited is known as the _____; the tract that is subject to the easement is called the _____.

11. An _____ is a personal right, such as that granted to utility companies to maintain poles, wires and pipelines.

12. A _____ is permission to enter another's property for a specific purpose.

13. An _____ is an unauthorized use of another's real estate.

14. The common-law doctrine of _____ rights applies to owners of land adjacent to navigable streams.

15. Owners of land bordering large lakes and oceans may be governed by the doctrine of _____ rights.

16. Under the doctrine of _____, water belongs to the state and is allocated to users who have obtained permits.

Key Term Matching, Part I

1. A state's ability to enact legislation to preserve order, protect the public health and safety and promote the general welfare

2. The right of a government to acquire privately owned real estate for public use

3. The process by which the government exercises its right of eminent domain

4. A charge imposed on real estate to raise funding for government services

5. The automatic transfer of real property to the state when the owner dies without heirs or a will

6. The degree, quantity, nature and extent of an owner's interest in real property

7. A class of estates that last for an indeterminable period of time

8. A class of estates that last for a fixed period of time

9. The highest interest in real estate recognized by law

10. An estate that is qualified by some action or activity that must not be performed

_____ condemnation

_____ eminent domain

_____ escheat

_____ estate in land

_____ fee simple absolute

_____ fee simple defeasible

_____ freehold estates

_____ leasehold estates

_____ police power

_____ taxation

Key Term Matching, Part II

1. The owner's right to retake possession of property through legal action if a limiting condition is broken

2. An estate based on the lifetime of a person other than the life tenant

3. The person to whom property passes when a life estate ends

4. A legal life estate in which an individual's primary residence is protected, in whole or in part, against certain creditors

5. Any claim, charge or liability that attaches to real estate

6. A charge against property that provides security for a debt or obligation of the property owner

7. A private agreement that affects the use of land

8. The right to use another's land for a particular purpose

9. All or part of a structure that extends beyond the land of its owner or beyond legal building lines

10. The doctrine that the right to use any water, with the exception of limited domestic uses, is held and controlled by the state

_____ deed restriction

_____ easement

_____ encroachment

_____ encumbrance

_____ homestead

_____ lien

_____ life estate pur autre vie

_____ prior appropriation

_____ remainderman

_____ right of reentry

True and False

_____ 1. A state's power to enact legislation that preserves order, protects the public health and safety and promotes the general welfare is referred to as its enabling act.

_____ 2. The four governmental powers that affect real estate are taxation, eminent domain, escheat and police.

_____ 3. The process by which the government exercises its right to acquire privately owned real estate for public use through either judicial or administrative proceedings is called eminent domain.

_____ 4. The purpose of escheat is to expand governmental property holdings.

_____ 5. A freehold estate is the highest interest in real estate recognized by law.

_____ 6. A conventional life estate may be created either by deed during the owner's life or after the owner's death by will.

_____ 7. If the grantor is silent about what happens to property after a life estate ends, the grantor has a remainder interest in the property.

_____ 8. A homestead is a legal life estate in real estate occupied as a family home.

_____ 9. An appurtenant easement is said to run with the land, and transfers with the deed of the servient tenement.

_____ 10. An easement that arises when an owner sells property that has no access to a street or public way except across the seller's remaining land is an easement by prescription.

_____ 11. The concept of "tacking" provides that successive periods of continuous occupation by different parties may be combined to reach the required total number of years necessary to establish a claim for an easement in gross.

_____ 12. A license may be terminated or canceled by the person who granted it, and ends on the death of either party or the sale of the affected property by the licensor.

_____ 13. Riparian rights are common-law rights granted to owners of land that lies along the course of a river, stream or similar body of water.

_____ 14. Riparian and littoral rights are personal rights under the common law: they belong to the landowner, and do not run with the land.

_____ 15. To secure water rights in a state in which the doctrine of prior appropriation is in effect, landowners must demonstrate that they plan a beneficial use for the water.

WRITE YOUR CORRECTIONS BELOW:

_____

_____

_____

_____

_____

_____

_____

_____

_____

_____

Multiple Choice

1. A life estate may be created by all of the following *EXCEPT* a:

   a. will.   c. deed.
   b. lease.   d. gift.

2. *J* and *S* are next-door neighbors. *S* asks *J* for permission to store a sailboat in *J*'s yard for a few weeks. *J* does not charge *S* rent for the use of the yard. *J* has given *S* a/an:

   a. easement appurtenant.
   b. easement by necessity.
   c. license.
   d. encroachment.

3. *F* conveyed a one-acre parcel of land to the Wee Fry Preschool. In the deed, *F* stated that the property was to be used only as a playground; *F* reserved a right of reentry. What kind of estate has *F* granted?

   a. Leasehold
   b. Fee simple subject to a condition subsequent
   c. Fee simple subject to a special limitation
   d. Freehold

4. *T* owns a farm that lies along the edge of the Brackish River, which is too shallow to be navigable. If *T* does not live in a jurisdiction that recognizes the doctrine of prior appropriation, how much (if any) of the river does *T* own?

   a. *T* owns the land to the edge of the river; the land under the river is owned by the state.
   b. *T* owns the land to the mean high water mark, and a right to apply for a water use permit.
   c. *T* owns the land up to the water's edge and the right to use the water.
   d. *T* owns the land under the river to the exact center of the waterway, and the right to use the water.

5. Over the past 15 years, the Brackish River has been slowly depositing soil along its eastern bank. As a result, the river is some 12 feet narrower than it used to be, and Rambling Acres, the property on the east side of the river, is now 12 feet larger than it used to be. This scenario is an example of which of the following processes?

   a. Reliction   c. Alluvion
   b. Erosion   d. Accretion

6. If the government acquires privately owned real estate through a condemnation suit, it is exercising its power of:

    a. escheat.   c. eminent domain.
    b. reverter.   d. defeasance.

7. *L* owned two acres. *L* sold one acre to *Q* and reserved an easement appurtenant for entrance and exit over *Q*'s acre to reach the public road. *Q*'s land:

    a. can be cleared of the easement if *Q* sells to a third party.
    b. is called the servient tenement.
    c. is called the dominant tenement.
    d. is subject to an easement in gross.

8. *N* owns a large island in the middle of a navigable river and a strip of land along the shore. *N* sells the strip on the river bank to the Granola County Canoe Club. For *N* to gain access to the island, *N* must claim by implication of law an easement:

    a. by necessity.
    b. in gross.
    c. by prescription.
    d. by restriction.

9. If the dominant estate merges with the servient estate, which of the following is true?

    a. The easement remains in effect for the entire parcel.
    b. The easement is suspended, but cannot be terminated.
    c. The easement is terminated.
    d. The new owner must bring a suit seeking severance of the easement from the combined properties.

10. In the state of New Freedonia, the homestead exemption is $15,000. Four years ago, *G*, a resident of New Freedonia, purchased a home for $58,500. *G* then fell on hard times. At a court-ordered sale, *G*'s property is purchased for $60,000. If *G* has an outstanding mortgage balance of $35,000 and other debts amounting to $24,360, how much is protected by the homestead exemption?

    a. $640   c. $15,000
    b. $2,140   d. $16,500

Illustration

In Figure 7.1, complete the Venn diagram by labeling each of the three circles with the three requirements for eminent domain. In Figure 7.2, each of the boxes represents one of the actors in the Spindley Acres conveyances. Read the facts, then write the name of the actor in the appropriate box. You also should identify how each person holds the property, and how it is conveyed from one to another. Finally, in Figure 7.3, fill in the table to reflect your state's statutory distributions.

Figure 7.1   **Requirements for Eminent Domain**

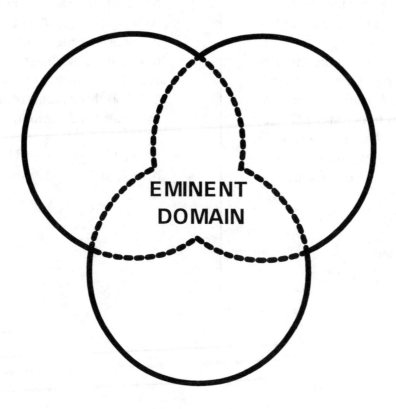

Figure 7.2   Who Owns Spindley Acres?

Ben conveys a life estate in Spindley Acres to Carol, with a remainder to Bob, "so long as Spindley Acres continues to be a working farm." If Spindley Acres ceases to be a farm, the property will go back to Ben (or his estate). Meanwhile, Carol conveys a life estate in Spindley Acres to Sally, "for so long as my Cousin Tom shall live." When Tom dies, the estate returns to Carol for the remainder of her life.

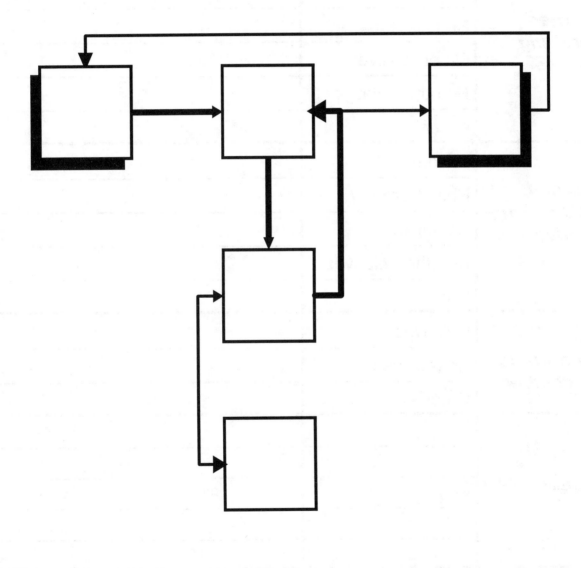

Figure 7.3 Statutory Distributions in the State of _____

DECEDENT STATUS	FAMILY STATUS	HOW PROPERTY PASSES
Married, surviving spouse	Children	
	No children	
	Other relatives	
	No other relatives	
	Other	
Married, no surviving spouse	Children	
	No Children	
	Relatives	
	No other relatives	
	Other	
Unmarried, no children	Relatives	
	No relatives	
	Other	
Other		

8 Forms of Real Estate Ownership

Chapter Summary

1. Ownership in _____ means that title is held by one natural person or legal entity.

2. In a _____, each party holds a separate, undivided interest, but shares possession with other tenants and each may sell his or her own individual interest.

3. _____ indicates two or more owners with the right of survivorship.

4. The four unities of _____, _____, _____ and _____ must be present in a joint tenancy.

5. Some states recognize a _____, which is actually a joint tenancy between a husband and wife.

6. In _____ states, property acquired by a husband and wife during their marriage are owned one-half by each, while property acquired prior to the marriage or by inheritance is considered separate property.

7. In a trust, the _____ conveys title to the _____, who owns and manages the property on behalf of the _____.

8. In a _____ form of ownership, owners hold a share in a

corporation or trust that operates the property.

9. _____ owners hold fee simple title to a unit, plus a share

of the common elements.

10. _____ enables multiple purchasers to own an estate or use

interest in real estate, with the right to occupy it for a part of each year.

Key Term Matching, Part I

1. Ownership of real estate by one individual	_____board of directors
2. A form of ownership in which each tenant holds an undivided fractional interest in the property	_____joint tenancy
	_____partition
3. A form of ownership in which multiple owners hold property with a right of survivorship	_____partnership
4. A legal method for dissolving a co-ownership	_____proprietary lease
5. A special form of co-ownership for married couples	_____severalty
6. A device by which one person transfers ownership of property to someone else to hold or manage for the benefit of a third party	_____tenancy by the entirety
	_____tenancy in common
7. A form of trust established by will after the owner's death	_____testamentary trust
	_____trust
8. An association of two or more persons who carry on a business for profit as co-owners	
9. The evidence of possession in a cooperative	
10. The governing body of a cooperative	

Key Term Matching, Part II

1. A business organization in which all members participate in the operation and management of the business and share full liability for business losses and obligations	_____ assessments
	_____ condo fee
	_____ condominium
2. A business organization that is a legal entity managed and operated by a board of directors	_____ corporation
3. A business organization in which two or more people or firms carry out a single business project	_____ general partnership
	_____ joint venture
4. A business organization that combines features of limited partnerships and corporations	_____ limited liability company
5. In a community property state, real or personal property that was owned solely by either spouse prior to marriage or acquired by inheritance during the marriage	_____ separate property
	_____ time-share estate
	_____ time-share use

6. A form of property ownership in which each owner holds an undivided interest in certain common elements in addition to holding his or her own property in fee simple

7. Special payments required of condominium unit owners to address specific expenses

8. Recurring fees required of condominium unit owners to cover basic maintenance and operations

9. A fee simple interest in a property that entitles the owner to use the facility for a certain period of time

10. A contract right under which a developer retains ownership of property and the purchaser receives the right to occupy and use the facilities for a certain period

True and False

_____ 1. There are three basic ways in which a fee simple estate may be held: in severalty, in co-ownership and in trust.

_____ 2. The term "severalty" means that there are several owners of a single property.

_____ 3. In a tenancy in common, title is held as though all owners collectively constitute a single common unit, with the right of survivorship.

_____ 4. The ownership of an undivided fractional interest in a property is characteristic of a tenancy in common.

_____ 5. A joint tenancy continues indefinitely, until there is only one remaining owner, who then holds title in entirety.

_____ 6. When title to a single parcel of real estate is held by two or more individuals, the parties may be referred to as "concurrent owners."

_____ 7. The four unities characteristic of a tenancy in common are possession, interest, title and time.

_____ 8. A joint tenant may freely convey his or her interest in the jointly held property to a new owner, who becomes a joint tenant.

_____ 9. A cotenancy may be terminated by asking a court to partition the property.

_____ 10. A tenancy by the entirety is a special form of ownership limited to married couples, although either spouse may freely convey his or her interest independently of the other.

_____ 11. A tenancy by the entirety may be terminated only by divorce or death.

_____ 12. In a community property state, "community property" includes all property, both real and personal, acquired by either party prior to or during the marriage.

_____ 13. The person who creates a trust is referred to as the "trustor."

_____ 14. In a general partnership, the death of one of the officers does not affect the organization's continuity.

_____ 15. When a corporation buys real property, the stockholders have a direct ownership interest in the real estate that is proportional to their stock interest.

_____ 16. A syndicate is a form of partnership in which two or more people or firms carry out a single business project, with no intention of establishing an ongoing or permanent relationship.

_____ 17. Condominium owners hold their own units in fee simple and the common elements under proprietary leases.

_____ 18. The management and operation of a cooperative are determined by the bylaws of the corporation that owns the property.

_____ 19. Ownership of a cooperative interest is personal property.

_____ 20. A time-share estate is a contract right.

WRITE YOUR CORRECTIONS BELOW:

_____

_____

_____

_____

_____

_____

_____

_____

_____

_____

_____

_____

_____

_____

_____

Multiple Choice

1. *P* and *J* own an apartment building together as joint tenants. They share equally in the expenses and profits. One day, *P* decides to end the relationship. If *P* sells her interest to *C* by signing and delivering a deed, which of the following statements is true?

   a. *C* will become a joint tenant with *J*.
   b. *C* and *J* will be tenants in common.
   c. *C* will be a tenant in common with *J* and a joint tenant with *P*.
   d. The conveyance will be invalid: *P* and *J* will remain joint tenants.

2. In February, *G* conveyed an undivided one-half interest in Sunny Orchard to *Q*. In March, *G* conveyed the remaining one-half interest to *R*. The deed to *R* included the following statement: "*R* is to be a joint tenant with *Q*." Both deeds were recorded. Based on these facts, which of the following statements is true?

   a. *Q* and *R* hold title to Sunny Orchard as joint tenants under the terms of the two conveyances from *G*.
   b. *Q* and *R* own Sunny Orchard by partition.
   c. *Q* and *R* are tenants in common.
   d. *R* owns Sunny Orchard as a joint tenant; *Q* owns Sunny Orchard as a tenant in common.

3. *E*, *F* and *G* own a large parcel of undeveloped land in joint tenancy. *E* wants to build a shopping center on the property, while *F* and *G* want to use it as an organic farm. *E* tries to buy the other tenant's interests, but they refuse. Which of the following is *E*'s best option?

   a. File a suit for partition
   b. Begin building a shopping center on one-third of the property
   c. Wait for *F* and *G* to die
   d. File a suit to quiet title

4. *T* owns a cottage in the Walden Acres community on the shore of Loon Lake. *T*'s ownership of the cottage is in fee simple. *T* also owns an undivided percentage interest in a parking lot, a golf course and a swimming pool, all located in the Walden Acres development. Because *T* is a school teacher in another state, *T* lives at Walden Acres only during the summer months. Based on these facts alone, *T*'s ownership is probably best described as a:

   a. time-share estate.
   b. time-share use.
   c. condominium.
   d. cooperative.

5. *P*, *Q* and *R* agree to purchase and operate Rickety Tower as a permanent investment. *P* and *Q* each contribute $50,000. *R* contributes $30,000 and agrees to run the day-to-day operations of the business, which they call "Rickety Tower Joint Venture Partners." Neither *P* nor *Q* has any right to participate in the operation of the venture. Based on these facts, what type of business organization have *P*, *Q* and *R* established?

   a. Joint venture
   b. Limited partnership
   c. General partnership
   d. Limited liability company

6. Based on the facts in the previous question, if Rickety Tower collapses, resulting in injury and property damage worth $275,000, what will be *P*'s liability?

   a. $0   c. $91,667
   b. $50,000   d. $100,000

7. All of the following are unities required for a joint tenancy *EXCEPT*:

   a. unity of title.
   b. unity of ownership.
   c. unity of time.
   d. unity of possession.

8. All of the following are characteristics of a tenancy by the entirety
   EXCEPT:

   a. title may be conveyed only by a
      deed signed by both parties.
   b. the surviving spouse automatically
      becomes sole owner of the
      property upon the death of the
      other spouse.
   c. each spouse owns an equal,
      undivided interest in the property
      as a single, indivisible unit.
   d. the surviving spouse automatically
      owns one-half of the property
      acquired during the marriage.

9. *N* creates a trust to pay for *M*'s real
   estate education. The trust is operated
   by *O*, who makes payments on *M*'s
   behalf directly to The Real Estate
   School. Based on these facts, which
   of the following statements best
   characterizes the relationships among
   these parties?

   a. *N* is the trustee, *M* is the
      beneficiary and *O* is the trustor.
   b. *N* is the trustor, *O* is the trustee
      and The Real Estate School is the
      beneficiary.
   c. *N* is the trustor, *M* is the
      beneficiary and *O* is the trustee.
   d. *N* is the trustor, *M* is the
      beneficiary, *O* is the trustee and
      The Real Estate School is the
      fiduciary.

10. *XYZ* is a legal entity, created by char-
    ter under the laws of the state of East
    Carolina. *XYZ* is managed and
    operated by a board, and is permitted
    to buy and sell real estate. When one
    of its directors dies, *XYZ* continues to
    operate. Because of its structure,
    XYZ's income is subject to double
    taxation. *XYZ* is best described as
    a/an:

    a. partnership.
    b. S corporation.
    c. corporation.
    d. limited liability company.

Illustration

*Next to each building in Figure 8.1 is a list of characteristics. First, label one building as a
condominium, one as a cooperative and one as a time share (it doesn't matter which ones you
choose). Then, strike out any characteristic in each list that does not apply to the type of
ownership you've assigned to each building.*

Figure 8.1   Types of Ownership

_____

corporate ownership

undivided interest in common elements

occupancy and use for limited periods

proprietary lease

fee simple ownership of units

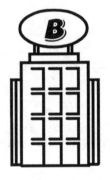

_____

corporate ownership

undivided interest in common elements

occupancy and use for limited periods

proprietary lease

fee simple ownership of units

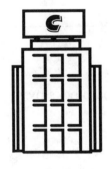

_____

corporate ownership

undivided interest in common elements

occupancy and use for limited periods

proprietary lease

fee simple ownership of units

9   Legal Descriptions

Chapter Summary

1. A _____ is a precise method of identifying a parcel of land.

2. Another term for a government survey is "_____ survey."

3. A _____ description uses direction and distance measurements to establish precise boundaries for a parcel, marked by monuments and fixed objects.

4. The _____ survey system surveys a parcel of land from only one principal meridian and its base line.

5. East and west lines parallel with the base line form six-mile-wide strips called _____ strips or tiers.

6. Townships are divided into _____ sections of one square mile each.

7. Land in every state can be subdivided into lots and blocks by means of a _____ map.

8. Air lots, condominium descriptions and other measurements of vertical elevations may be computed from the United States Geological Survey _____.

Key Term Matching

1. The type of legal description that relies on a property's physical features to describe and determine the boundaries and measurements of the parcel

2. The designated starting point for a metes-and-bounds description

3. Fixed objects used to identify significant points of measurement in a metes-and-bounds description

4. A land description system based on principal meridians and base lines

5. Lines of measurement that run north and south

6. Lines of measurement that run east and west

7. Lines running six miles apart and parallel to the base line

8. Strips of land running parallel to the meridian

9. A device to compensate for inaccurate measurements and the shape of the earth

10. Undersized or oversized sections

11. A system of description that uses numbers referred to in a plat map

12. A point, line or surface from which elevations are measured

13. Permanent reference points, usually found on embossed brass markers set in concrete or asphalt bases, used for marking datums.

_____ base lines

_____ benchmarks

_____ correction lines

_____ datum

_____ fractional sections

_____ lot-and-block

_____ metes-and-bounds

_____ monuments

_____ POB

_____ principal meridians

_____ ranges

_____ rectangular survey system

_____ township lines

True and False

_____ 1. The metes-and-bounds description was established by Congress in 1785.

_____ 2. In the metes-and-bounds system, a monument may be either a natural object or a man-made marker.

_____ 3. Principal meridians run east and west.

_____ 4. Township lines and base lines are parallel.

_____ 5. Ranges are strips of land six miles wide that run parallel to the base line.

_____ 6. When the horizontal township lines and the vertical range lines intersect, they form township squares.

_____ 7. Every township contains 36 sections of 64 acres each.

_____ 8. Section 6 is always in the northeast or upper left-hand corner.

_____ 9. In the rectangular survey system, a comma may be used in place of the word "and."

_____ 10. Areas smaller than a full quarter-section are designated as fractional sections.

_____ 11. A datum is a permanent reference point, usually found on an embossed brass marker set into a solid concrete or asphalt base.

_____ 12. Air lots are composed of the airspace within specific boundaries located over a parcel of land.

WRITE YOUR CORRECTIONS BELOW:

_____

_____

_____

_____

_____

_____

_____

_____

_____

_____

_____

Multiple Choice

1. Which of the following most accurately describes a quarter section?

   a. ¼ mile by ¼ mile
   b. ½ mile by ½ mile
   c. ½ mile by 1 mile
   d. ⅛ mile by ⅛ mile

2. If a parcel described as the NW 1/4 of the SE 1/4 of Section 10, T2N, R3W of the 4th P.M. is sold for $500 per acre, what will be the sale price of the parcel?

   a. $16,000   c. $40,000
   b. $20,000   d. $82,500

3. How many acres are contained in a parcel described as follows: *The NE 1/4 of the NW 1/4; the N 1/2 of the NW 1/4, NE 1/4, Section 10?*

   a. 40 acres   c. 70 acres
   b. 60 acres   d. 74 acres

4. *K* sells six acres of prime unde-veloped property to *L* for $2.25 per square foot. How much did *L* pay?

   a. $466,560   c. $612,360
   b. $588,060   d. $733,860

5. Which township section number is directly north of Section 7?

   a. Section 1   c. Section 5
   b. Section 6   d. Section 8

Answer questions 6 through 12 by referring to the plat of Honeysuckle Hills in Figure 9.1.

6. Which lot in Block A has the most frontage on Jasmine Lane?

   a. 1   c. 7
   b. 2   d. 11

7. How many lots have easements?

   a. 1   c. 4
   b. 3   d. 6

8. Which road or roads run east and west?

   a. Wolf and Jasmine
   b. Carney and Goodrich
   c. Wolf only
   d. Goodrich only

9. If lots 13 and 14 were to be combined into a single parcel, how many square feet would it contain?

   a. 1,020   c. 22,800
   b. 19,800   d. 21,600

10. *Beginning at the intersection of the West line of Carney Street and the North line of Wolf Road, running west 140 feet, then North 120 feet, then North 50 degrees East 120 feet, then following the southeasterly curvature of the South line of Jasmine Lane for 100 feet, then South 120 feet to POB.*

    To which lot does this description refer?

    a. Lot 15, Block B
    b. Lot 8, Block A
    c. Lots 7, 8 and 9, Block A
    d. Lots 8 and 9, Block A

11. Which lot has the least street exposure?

    a. Lot 3, Block A
    b. Lot 15, Block B
    c. Lot 9, Block A
    d. Lot 10, Block B

12. Assume the bold number *14* is in the exact middle of lot 14, Block B, and represents the location of a monument. The monument marks the northeast corner of a subdivided rectangular parcel. If the parcel is bounded by Jasmine Lane and Lots 13, 14 and 15, approximately how many square feet is the subdivided parcel?

    a. 1,210   c. 4,500
    b. 2,700   d. 5,400

Illustration

Figure 9.1 is a map of Honeysuckle Hills subdivision

Figure 9.1

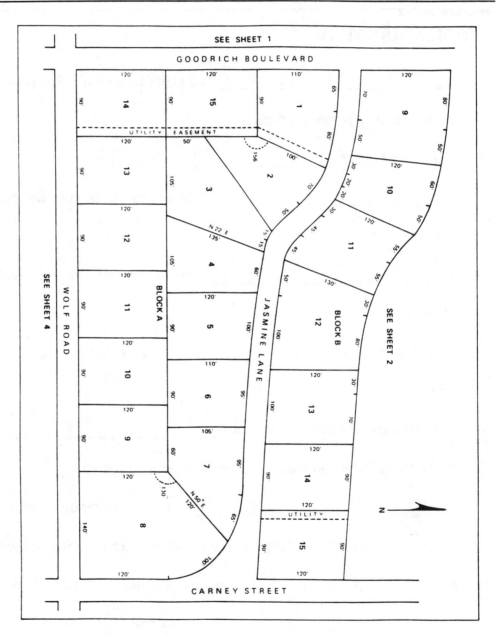

10

Real Estate Taxes and Other Liens

Chapter Summary

1. A _____ is a claim by a creditor or taxing authority against a debtor's real or personal property.

2. A lien is a type of _____.

3. A _____ lien covers all the real and personal property of a debtor/owner.

4. A _____ lien covers only certain identified property of a debtor/owner.

5. Liens that arise from the debtor's own actions are referred to as _____ liens.

6. Liens that are imposed by statute are _____ liens.

7. A lien that is based on the concept of fairness is called an _____ lien.

8. The _____ of liens is generally determined by the order in which they are placed in the public record of the county in which the property is located.

9. Some states permit a certain time period during which a defaulted owner may _____ his or her real estate from a tax sale.

10. _____ are levied to allocate the cost of public improvements to the owners of the specific parcels that benefit.

11. A _____ lien is a voluntary, specific lien held by a mortgage lender to secure payment for a real estate loan.

12. A general contractor, subcontractor or material supplier whose work enhances the value of real estate is protected by a _____ lien.

13. A _____ is a court decree obtained by a creditor, usually for a monetary award from a debtor.

14. A means of preventing a defendant from conveying property before completion of a suit in which a judgment is sought is _____.

15. A _____ is a recorded notice of a lawsuit that is pending in court and that may affect title to a parcel of real estate.

16. State _____ taxes are general liens against a deceased owner's property.

17. Corporation franchise tax liens are general liens against a corporation's _____.

18. Internal Revenue Service tax liens are _____ liens against the property of a person who is delinquent in his or her federal taxes.

Key Term Matching, Part I

1. A charge or claim against a person's property, to enforce the payment of money

2. A lien that is created intentionally by the property owner's action

3. A lien created by law

4. A lien that arises out of common law

5. A lien that affects all the real and personal property owned by a debtor

6. A lien that is secured by certain property

7. The order in which claims against property will be satisfied

8. A written agreement between lienholders to change the priority of a lien

9. Charges imposed by state and local governments to fund their functions and services

10. A general real estate tax

_____ ad valorum

_____ equitable lien

_____ general lien

_____ involuntary lien

_____ lien

_____ priority

_____ specific lien

_____ subordination

_____ taxes

_____ voluntary lien

Key Term Matching, Part II

1. The official process of valuing real estate for tax purposes	_____assessment
2. A device to achieve uniformity in statewide assessments	_____attachment
3. 1/1,000 of a dollar, or $.001	_____equalization factor
4. The right of a delinquent taxpayer to recover property before a tax sale	_____equitable right of redemption
5. The right of a delinquent taxpayer to recover property after a tax sale	_____lis pendens
6. Taxes levied on specific properties that benefit from public improvements	_____mechanic's lien
7. A specific, involuntary lien that gives security to persons or companies who perform labor or furnish material to improve real property	_____mill
8. A court decree that establishes the amount owed by a debtor and provides for money to be awarded	_____money judgment
9. A notice of a possible future lien based on a lawsuit	_____special assessments
10. A writ that permits a court to retain custody of a debtor's property until the creditor's lawsuit is concluded	_____statutory right of redemption

True and False

_____ 1. A voluntary lien may be classified as either statutory or equitable.

_____ 2. A charge or claim against a person's property by a creditor, made to enforce the payment of money, is referred to as a lien.

_____ 3. All encumbrances are liens.

_____ 4. Taking out a mortgage loan is an example of the creation of an equitable lien.

_____ 5. Both federal estate taxes and state inheritance taxes are general, statutory and involuntary liens.

_____ 6. A lien attaches to real property at the time the lien is filed.

_____ 7. A special assessment is always a specific, statutory and involuntary lien.

_____ 8. A court's decree that establishes the amount owed by a debtor is enforced by a judgment directing the sheriff to seize and sell the debtor's property.

_____ 9. Mechanics' liens never take priority over tax or special assessment liens.

_____ 10. "Ad valorem" taxes apply to the difference between the assessed value of a property and the value added by resale or improvement.

_____ 11. All liens are encumbrances.

_____ 12. The presence of a lien on real property does not prevent the owner from conveying title to another party.

_____ 13. A taxing body determines the appropriate tax rate by dividing the total monies needed for the coming fiscal year by the total assessments of all real estate located within the taxing body's jurisdiction.

_____ 14. A delinquent taxpayer may redeem property at any time prior to a tax sale by exercising his or her statutory right of redemption.

_____ 15. A mechanic's lien is a specific, involuntary lien.

WRITE YOUR CORRECTIONS BELOW:

_____

_____

_____

_____

_____

_____

_____

_____

_____

_____

_____

_____

_____

Multiple Choice

1. *C* stopped making mortgage payments to *M* in June. In February, *C* contracted with *B* to have his billiard room converted into a sauna, and never paid for the work. *C* is two years delinquent in property taxes to the village of *V*, and owes more than $30,000 on a custom luxury automobile purchased from *D* in January. *C*'s state gives mechanics' liens priority. If all these creditors obtain judgments against *C* in November, what will be the priority of their liens?

    a. 1. *D*, 2. *B*, 3. *M*, 4. *V*
    b. 1. *V*, 2. *M*, 3. *B*, 4. *D*
    c. 1. *B*, 2. *V*, 3. *D*, 4. *M*
    d. 1. *V*, 2. *B*, 3. *M*, 4. *D*

2. The town of Racoon's Paw wants to construct new concrete curbs in a residential neighborhood. How will the town most likely raise the money necessary for the improvement?

    a. Ad valorem tax
    b. Special assessment
    c. Equalized assessment
    d. Utility lien

3. All of the following liens must be recorded *EXCEPT:*

    a. money judgment.
    b. mechanic's lien.
    c. real estate tax lien.
    d. voluntary lien.

4. The market value of an undeveloped parcel is $20,000. Its assessed value is 40 percent of market value, and properties in its county are subject to an equalization factor of 1.50. If the tax rate is $4 per $100, what is the amount of the tax owed on the property?

    a. $320   c. $800
    b. $480   d. $1,200

5. All of the following are liens against real property *EXCEPT:*

    a. a mortgage.
    b. real estate taxes.
    c. lis pendens.
    d. secured debts of a deceased property owner.

6. A real estate tax is a:

    a. specific, involuntary lien.
    b. specific, voluntary lien.
    c. general, involuntary lien.
    d. general, voluntary lien.

7. Which of the following may be either an involuntary or a voluntary lien on real property?

    a. Mortgage loan
    b. Real estate tax
    c. Special assessment
    d. Mechanic's lien

8. *G* was considering having a new garage built. *G* talked about the project with several contractors, including *Y*. In April, while *G* was on vacation, *Y* began building the garage according to *G*'s specifications. Work was completed by the end of May. In June, *G* returned from vacation, and refused to pay for the garage. *Y* decides to file a mechanic's lien in July. Is *Y* entitled to a lien?

    a. Yes, because the garage was constructed according to *G*'s specifications.
    b. Yes, because the garage is not a part of an owner-occupied residence.
    c. No, because notice of the lien should have been filed in May, when the work was completed.
    d. No, because there was no express or implied contract between *G* and *Y*.

9. Which of the following would permit a law enforcement officer to seize a debtor's property?

    a. Lis pendens
    b. Satisfaction of judgment
    c. Writ of execution
    d. Writ of attachment

10. If the property owners in the Peachtree Hills neighborhood petition the city for new sidewalks and repaved alleys, which of the following best describes the character of the lien that may result if the city agrees to the improvements?

    a. General, statutory and voluntary
    b. Specific, equitable and involuntary
    c. Specific, statutory and voluntary
    d. General, equitable and involuntary

11. Which of the following is a general, statutory and involuntary lien on both real and personal property?

    a. Federal tax lien
    b. Mechanic's lien
    c. Special assessment
    d. Consumer loan lien

12. All of the following may be specific, statutory and involuntary liens *EXCEPT* a:

    a. bail bond lien.
    b. special assessment lien.
    c. municipal utility lien.
    d. mechanic's lien.

Illustration

In Figure 10.1, each box is labeled with a characteristics of different types of liens. Write the number of each lien from the list in ALL *the boxes that describe that lien's characteristics.*

Figure 10.1   **Liens**

GENERAL	INVOLUNTARY	STATUTORY

EQUITABLE

1 Mechanic's Lien
2 Special Assessment
3 Mortgage
4 Bail Bond
5 Utility Lien
6 Federal Estate Tax
7 Corporation Franchise Tax
8 State Inheritance Tax
9 Judgment
10 Real Estate Tax

SPECIFIC

VOLUNTARY

KEY
203

11 Real Estate Contracts

Chapter Summary

1. A contract is a legally enforceable _____.

2. A written contract that establishes the parties' intentions is referred to as a/an

   _____ contract.

3. A _____ contract is one in which both parties have

   obligated themselves to act.

4. An _____ contract is one that has been fully performed.

5. A contract that has not been completely performed is an _____ contract.

6. To be _____, a real estate contract must include a

   description of the property.

7. The act of transferring one party's rights or obligations by substituting a new contract is

   called a _____.

8. If either party to a contract suffers a loss due to the other party's default, the injured

   party may sue to recover _____.

9. A contract that gives one party the exclusive right, for a specific period of time, to

   purchase or lease a property is an _____.

10. Under a _____ contract, the buyer takes possession of and

responsibility for the property, but does not receive the deed immediately.

Key Term Matching, Part I

1. A voluntary, legally enforceable promise between legally competent parties

2. A contract in which the parties show their intention in words

3. A contract established by the acts and conduct of the parties

4. A contract in which both parties promise to perform some act

5. A one-sided agreement

6. A contract that has been completely performed

7. The status of a real estate sales contract prior to closing

8. The person who accepts the offer in a contract

9. Complete agreement about the purpose and terms of a contract

10. Something of legal value offered by one party and accepted by another as an inducement to act or refrain from acting

_____ bilateral contract

_____ consideration

_____ contract

_____ executed contract

_____ executory contract

_____ express contract

_____ implied contract

_____ mutual assent

_____ offeree

_____ unilateral contract

Key Term Matching, Part II

1. A contract that is without legal force or effect

2. The transfer of rights or duties under a contract

3. The substitution of a new contract to replace an earlier one

4. A violation of any of the terms or conditions of a contract without legal excuse

5. An employment contract between a broker and a seller

6. A deposit customarily made by a prospective purchaser when making an offer

7. The interest held by a buyer prior to delivery and acceptance of the deed

8. An amount of money that the parties agree will be the complete compensation available in the event of a breach

9. Additional conditions that must be satisfied before a sales contract is fully enforceable

10. A contract under which the seller retains title to property but the buyer obtains possession

_____ assignment

_____ breach

_____ contingencies

_____ earnest money

_____ equitable title

_____ land contract

_____ liquidated damages

_____ listing agreement

_____ novation

_____ void

True and False

_____ 1. An agreement to be bound by most of the terms proposed in an offer constitutes acceptance.

_____ 2. All contracts must be in writing to be enforceable.

_____ 3. A listing agreement is a contract for the sale of real estate.

_____ 4. Consideration is something of legal value offered by one party and accepted by the other as an inducement to act.

_____ 5. In an implied contract, the actual agreement between the parties is inferred from general or vague statements in the written agreement itself.

_____ 6. The difference between a bilateral and a unilateral contract is the number of parties involved.

_____ 7. A sales contract is an executory contract from the time it is signed until closing; at closing, it becomes an executed contract.

_____ 8. A contract that may be rescinded or disaffirmed by one or both of the parties based on some legal principle is void, even though it may appear on the surface to be valid.

_____ 9. The person who makes an offer is the offeree; the person who accepts or rejects the offer is the offeror.

_____ 10. A contract entered into by a mentally ill person is voidable during the illness and for some time after the individual is cured.

_____ 11. An oral agreement for the sale of real estate is unenforceable.

_____ 12. Under a land contract, the buyer obtains both possession and title to the property by agreeing to make regular monthly payments to the seller over a number of years.

_____ 13. Assignment is the substitution of a new contract in place of the original one, while novation is a transfer of rights or duties under a contract.

_____ 14. An offer or counteroffer may be revoked at any time prior to its acceptance.

_____ 15. An option contract is an agreement by which the optionee gives the optionor the right to buy or lease property at a fixed price within a specific period of time.

_____ 16. Commingling occurs when a broker mixes his or her personal funds with a buyer's earnest money deposit.

_____ 17. The interest held by a buyer during the time between the signing of a sales contract and the transfer of title is known as equitable title.

_____ 18. An addendum is an additional, new provision that is added to an existing contract without altering the content of the original.

_____ 19. An option agreement is a unilateral contract.

_____ 20. A contract entered into by a minor is void.

WRITE YOUR CORRECTIONS BELOW:

_____

_____

_____

_____

_____

_____

_____

_____

_____

_____

_____

Multiple Choice

1. *P*, a real estate broker, announces to the salespeople in her office that she will pay a $1,000 bonus to the top-selling salesperson each quarter. This contract is a/an:

   a. implied bilateral contract.
   b. express unilateral contract.
   c. implied unilateral contract.
   d. express bilateral contract.

2. *G* makes an offer on a house, and *R*, the seller, accepts. What is the *current status* of this relationship?

   a. *G* and *R* do not have a valid contract until *R* delivers title at closing.
   b. *G* and *R* have an express, bilateral executed contract.
   c. *G* and *R* have an express, bilateral executory contract.
   d. *G* and *R* have an implied, unilateral executory contract.

3. *F* offers to buy *M*'s house for the full $95,000 asking price. The offer contains the following clause: "Possession of the premises on August 1." *M* is delighted to accept *F*'s offer, and signs the contract. First, however, *M* crosses out "August 1" and replaces it with "August 3," because *M* won't be back from vacation on the first of the month. *M* then begins scheduling movers. What is the status of this agreement?

   a. Because *M*'s change was minor, *F* and *M* have a valid contract.
   b. *M* has accepted *F*'s offer: the change is of no legal effect once the contract has been signed.
   c. *M* has rejected *F*'s offer and made a counteroffer, which *F* is free to accept or reject.
   d. While *M* technically rejected *F*'s offer, *M*'s behavior in scheduling movers creates an implied contract between the parties.

4. A contract that is entered into by a person who is under the age of contractual capacity is:

   a. unenforceable.   c. voidable.
   b. void.   d. valid.

5. *Q* and *B* enter into an oral agreement for the sale of Halfacre Farm. *B* changes his mind, and *Q* suffers a financial loss of $1,500. Which of the following best describes *Q*'s position?

   a. *Q* may sue *B* for specific performance under the statute of frauds, forcing the sale of Halfacre Farm.
   b. *Q* may sue *B* to recover the $1,500 loss, but may not compel *B* to perform.
   c. *Q* has no legal remedy, because this transaction should have been in writing as required by the statute of frauds.
   d. *Q* may sue for specific performance, but may not sue to recover monetary damages alone.

6. On March 7, *N* and *L* execute a contract for the purchase of *N*'s property. Closing is set for June 10. On April 15, the property is struck by lightning and virtually destroyed by the resulting fire. If the Uniform Vendor and Purchaser Risk Act has been adopted by the state in which the property is located, which party bears liability for the loss?

   a. *N* and *L* share the loss equally under the Act.
   b. *N* bears the loss alone.
   c. *L* bears the loss alone, by virtue of her equitable title.
   d. Neither *N* nor *L* bears the loss.

7. *T* is buying *K*'s house, and agrees to assume *K*'s mortgage. The lender agrees and releases *K* from the obligation, substituting *T* as the party primarily liable for the debt. Which of the following terms best describes this transaction?

   a. Assignment
   b. Novation
   c. Conversion
   d. Consideration

8. *R* is trying to sell Dreadful Manor, but is having difficulty finding a buyer. *H* wants to buy Dreadful Manor but isn't sure whether or not she will be transferred out of the country by her employer. *R* agrees to accept a $500 payment from *H*, in return for which Dreadful Manor will be taken off the market for three months. *H* may purchase Dreadful Manor for a certain price any time during that period. This is a/an:

   a. unenforceable contract.
   b. land contract.
   c. sales contract.
   d. option contract.

9. All the following are essential to a valid real estate sales contract *EXCEPT:*

   a. a written agreement, signed by both parties.
   b. consideration.
   c. an earnest money deposit, held in an escrow account.
   d. legally competent parties.

10. A 14 year-old comes into a brokerage office and says, "I want to make an offer on the Walnut Street property. Here is a certified check for 10 percent of the asking price. Please help me with the paperwork." Why should the broker be concerned?

   a. A contract for the sale of real estate in which one of the parties is a minor is illegal.
   b. The earnest money deposit must be at least 20 percent of the asking price when a minor is involved in the transaction.
   c. The sales contract may be disaffirmed by the minor when he or she reaches the age of majority.
   d. The sales contract will be void because the minor's age is a matter of public record.

Illustration

Figure 11.1 is the first page of a standard real estate sales contract. Fill it in, based on the following information: You are the buyer. The date is today. The property is 1105 Azalea Street in Poleduck County, city of Pleasant Valley, East Virginia 98765. The lot dimensions are 70 by 160 feet. The sellers are Paul and Polly Purveyor, who currently live in the house being sold. The buyer is particularly insistent that the kitchen appliances (a stove, dishwasher and refrigerator) convey with the property, and that an outdoor gas cooker and swingset stay as well. The earnest money deposit is 15 percent of the purchase price of $117,500, paid by check, with an additional 10 percent of the balance due in one business week. The closing will take place exactly 64 days from today at the office of the buyer's attorney, R. Tassel. The financing will be by conventional, fixed-rate mortgage, in the amount of the balance due. The buyer will not accept an interest rate greater than 7.5 percent. The commitment date is two weeks from today. The listing broker is F. J. Broker.

Figure 11.1   Sample Residential Sales Contract

BUYER(S),_____

Address_____;

City _____State _____; Zip_____agrees to purchase, and

SELLER(S):_____

Address:_____; City _____

State_____; Zip _____ agrees to sell to Buyer(s) at the

Price of _____ Dollars ($_____)

the Property commonly described as _____

(City of _____, County of _____,

State of _____), "the Property," a complete legal descrip-
tion of which may be attached to this contract by either party. The Property has approx-imate lot
dimensions of _____, together with all existing improvements and
fixtures, if any, to be transferred to the Buyer(s) by Bill of Sale at the time of closing, in-cluding
(but not limited to): hot water heater, furnace, plumbing and electrical fixtures, sump pumps,
central heating and cooling, central heating and cooling systems, fixed floor coverings, built-in
kitchen appliances and cabinets, storm and screen windows and doors, window treat-ment
hardware, shelving systems, all planted vegetation, garage door openers and car units, and the
following items of personal property:

2. EARNEST MONEY: Buyer has paid $_____ by check by note *(circle
one)*, and will pay within _____ days the further sum of $_____, as earnest money to
be applied against the purchase price. The earnest money shall be held by the Listing Broker
for the mutual benefit of the parties. The balance of the purchase price, $_____, shall be
paid in full at closing.

3. CLOSING DATE: The closing date shall be _____, 19__, at _____.

4. POSSESSION: Possession shall be at closing.

5. COMMISSION: Seller(s) agree that _____, Listing Broker, brought
about this sale and agrees to pay a Broker's commission as agreed in the listing agreement.

6. FINANCING: This contract is subject to the condition that Buyer(s) shall, by _____, 19 __,
obtain a written commitment for a loan secured by a mortgage or deed of trust on the Property
in the amount of $_____. Financing shall be secured in the form of a mortgage
of the following type:*(delete those items that do not apply)* Conventional (fixed or adjustable
rate); FHA mortgage; VA mortgage; assumption of existing mortgage; financing by Seller(s).

12 Transfer of Title

Chapter Summary

1. _____Title_____ to real estate is the right to and evidence of ownership of the land.

2. The _____Voluntary_____ transfer of an owner's title is made by a deed, executed by the owner as grantor to the purchaser or donee as grantee.

3. A deed should be properly _____acknowledged_____ before a notary public.

4. A deed must contain a _____Granting_____ clause that states the grantor's intention to convey the property.

5. Title is said to pass only when a deed is _____delivered_____.

6. A _____General_____ warranty deed provides the greatest protection.

7. A _____Special_____ warranty deed warrants that the grantor received title and that the property was not encumbered during the time he or she held title.

8. A _____Bargain & Sale_____ deed implies that the grantor holds title and possession but contains no express warranties.

9. A _____Quitclaim_____ deed provides the grantee with the least protection of any deed.

10. The gift of real property by will is known as a ___Devise___ .

11. ___Probate___ is a formal judicial process that proves or confirms

the validity of a will, determines the deceased person's assets and identifies the persons

to whom the property passes.

12. Land may be acquired through the natural process of ___accretion___ .

Key Term Matching, Part I

1. The right to and evidence of ownership of land

2. The transfer of title by gift or sale

3. A written instrument by which an owner conveys the right, title or interest in a parcel of real estate to someone else

4. The person who transfers title

5. The person who acquires title by gift or sale

6. A statement of the intention to convey property by deed

7. A formal declaration, made before a notary public, that the person who is signing the deed is doing so voluntarily and that his or her signature is genuine

8. A covenant that the grantor is the owner of the property and has the right to convey it

9. A guarantee that the grantee's title will be good against any third party who might bring legal action to establish superior title

10. A conveyance by deed from a trustor to a trustee

___7___ acknowledgment

___3___ deed

___10___ deed in trust

___5___ grantee

___6___ granting clause

___4___ grantor

___9___ quiet enjoyment

___8___ seisin

___1___ title

___2___ voluntary alienation

Key Term Matching, Part II

1. A type of deed that warrants only that the grantor received title, and that the property has not been encumbered during the grantor's ownership

2. A deed that contains no express warranties, but that implies that the grantor holds title and possession of the property

3. A deed that contains no covenants, warranties or implications and that provides the least protection of any deed

4. A conveyance by deed from a trustee to anyone other than the trustor

5. A conveyance by deed from a trustee to the trustor

6. The transfer of title without the owner's consent

7. Having prepared a will indicating how property is to be disposed of after death

8. The gift of real property by will

9. The person who makes a will

10. A formal judicial process to confirm a will's validity

___2___ bargain and sale

___8___ devise

___6___ involuntary alienation

___10__ probate

___3___ quitclaim

___5___ reconveyance deed

___1___ special warranty

___7___ testate

___9___ testator

___4___ trustee's deed

True and False

_____ 1. A title to real estate is a printed document signed by the secretary of state.

_____ 2. A deed is the written instrument by which an owner of real estate intentionally conveys the right, title or interest in a parcel to someone else.

_____ 3. To be valid, a deed must include a recital of consideration, an identifiable grantee and a recital of exceptions and reservations.

_____ 4. A title is considered transferred when the deed is actually signed and acknowledged by the grantor.

_____ 5. To be valid, a deed must be signed by both the grantor and the grantee.

_____ 6. In a special warranty deed, the covenant of seisin warrants that the grantor's title will be good against third parties.

_____ 7. In a general warranty deed, the covenant of further assurance represents a promise by the grantor that he or she will obtain and deliver any instrument needed to ensure good title.

_____ 8. A bargain and sale deed does not contain any express warranties against encumbrances.

_____ 9. If a trustee wanted to convey real estate back to the grantor, he or she would use a trustee's deed.

_____ 10. In a deed executed pursuant to court order, the full amount of consideration is stated in the deed.

_____ 11. Adverse possession is an example of involuntary alienation of property.

_____ 12. When a property owner dies, his or her heirs by descent or will may immediately take possession of any real estate.

_____ 13. While a deed must be delivered during the grantor's lifetime, a will takes effect only after the owner's death.

_____ 14. A person who receives real property through a testamentary transfer is referred to as the devisee.

_____ 15. Real property of an owner who dies intestate is distributed according to the laws of the state in which the owner resided at the time of his or her death.

WRITE YOUR CORRECTIONS BELOW:

_____

_____

Multiple Choice

1. *F* conveys Happy Acres to *R* by a written document that contains five covenants protecting *R*'s title. What is *F*'s role in this transaction?

   a. Grantee   c. Devisor
   b. Grantor   d. Devisee

2. All of the following are necessary to a valid deed *EXCEPT:*

   a. recital of consideration.
   b. words of conveyance.
   c. grantee's signature.
   d. delivery.

3. *I, M, hereby convey to my nearest relative all my interest in the property known as 123 Main Street, Elkhorn, West Dakota, to have and to hold, in consideration of receipt of the amount of $10 and other good and valuable consideration. Signed,* M.

   Which of the following statements is true regarding this conveyance?

   a. It is a valid conveyance by deed.
   b. It is an invalid conveyance by deed, because the property conveyed is inadequately described.
   c. It is an invalid conveyance by deed, because there is no recital of exceptions and reservations.
   d. It is an invalid conveyance by deed, because the grantee is inadequately identified.

4. The type of deed that imposes the least liability on a grantor is a:

   a. special warranty deed.
   b. bargain and sale deed.
   c. quitclaim deed.
   d. general warranty deed.

5. Title is not considered transferred until the deed is:

   a. signed by the grantor.
   b. delivered to and accepted by the grantee.
   c. delivered to the grantee.
   d. released from escrow.

6. Which of the following is a guarantee that the grantor has the right to convey the property?

   a. Covenant against encumbrances
   b. Covenant of seisin
   c. Covenant of further assurance
   d. Covenant of quiet enjoyment

7. A bargain and sale deed contains how many express warranties?

   a. 0   c. 3
   b. 2   d. 5

8. Which type of deed is used primarily to convey less than a fee simple estate?

   a. Bargain-and-sale deed
   b. Special warranty deed
   c. General warranty deed
   d. Quitclaim deed

9. *T* inherited Stately Manor from his uncle in 1975. *T* has never visited Stately Manor or taken any responsibility for it. In 1978, without *T*'s knowledge, *L* moved into the empty house. Between 1978 and 1992, *L* repaired and maintained Stately Manor as if it were her own home. She invited neighbors to attend holiday parties on the grounds. In 1992, *L* moved out of Stately Manor, and her son moved in. If the applicable period for adverse possession is 15 years, when can *L*'s son claim title?

   a. *L*'s son can claim title by adverse possession in the year 2007.
   b. *L*'s son cannot claim title, because *L* failed to satisfy the requirements for adverse possession.
   c. *L*'s son can claim title on the 15th anniversary of the date when *L* moved into Stately Manor.
   d. *L*'s son cannot claim title, because *T* is the true legal owner of Stately Manor.

10. Under the law of the state of North Michigan, ½ of an intestate decedent's property goes to his or her spouse, ¼ of the remainder is divided equally among his or her children, and ¼ goes to the state. If there is no spouse, the children divide ¾ equally. *K*, a citizen of North Michigan, dies intestate, survived by an ex-spouse and seven adult children. If *K*'s estate is $865,550, how much will each child receive under North Michigan law?

   a. $0
   b. $92,737.50
   c. $61,825.00
   d. $123,650.00

11. In East Carolina, the transfer tax is $1.20 for each $300 (or fraction of $300) of the sales price of any parcel of real estate. If a seller's property sold for $250,000, what will be the amount of the transfer tax due?

   a. $999.60
   b. $999.99
   c. $1,000.80
   d. $1,250.50

12. In front of witnesses, *G* says to *R*, "I never made a will, but I want you to have The Quarteracre Farm when I die." If *R* becomes the owner of The Quarteracre Farm, it is because the state recognizes what kind of will?

   a. Holographic
   b. Testamentary
   c. Nuncupative
   d. Probated

Illustration

Use Figure 12.1 to create a bar chart illustrating the characteristics of different types of deeds. Fill in the boxes above each type where the characteristic listed on the left side of the grid is a necessary component of the deed or is characteristic of it. When you're done, you can compare the relative protections of each kind of deed. In Figure 12.2, write the type of deed used for these conveyances: **trustor to trustee, trustee to beneficiary,** *and* **trustee to trustor**.

Figure 12.1   Characteristics of Deeds

	GENERAL WARRANTY DEED	SPECIAL WARRANTY DEED	BARGAIN ANDSALE DEED	QUIT-CLAIM DEED
COVENANT OF WARRANTY FOREVER				
COVENANT OF FURTHER ASSURANCE				
COVENANT OF QUIET ENJOYMENT				
COVENANT AGAINST ENCUMBRANCES				
COVENANT OF SEISIN				
EXPRESS WARRANTIES				
IMPLIED WARRANTIES				
DELIVERY AND ACCEPTANCE				
LEGAL DESCRIPTION				
HABENDUM CLAUSE				
GRANTING CLAUSE				
IDENTIFIABLE GRANTEE				
SIGNATURE OF GRANTOR				
CONSIDERATION				
GRANTOR OF SOUND MIND				
GRANTOR OF LAWFUL AGE				
↕CHARACTERISTICS / TYPE OF DEED↔	GENERAL WARRANTY DEED	SPECIAL WARRANTY DEED	BARGAIN ANDSALE DEED	QUIT-CLAIM DEED

Figure 12.2   **Types of Trust Deeds**

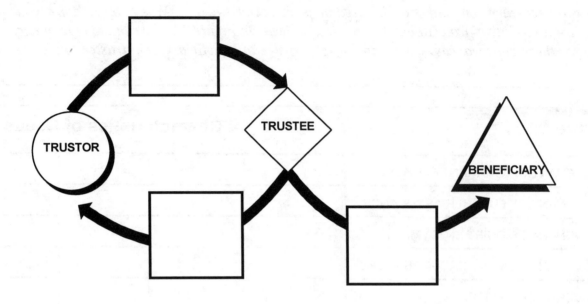

13   Title Records

Chapter Summary

1. The purpose of recording acts is to give interested parties legal, public and constructive

    _____ of an individual's interests in a property.

2. _____ is the act of placing documents in the public record.

3. Properly recording documents in the public record serves as _____

    notice to the world of an individual's rights or interest in property.

4. A person who has searched the public records and inspected a property is considered to

    have _____ notice of information relevant to the property.

5. _____ refers to the order of rights in time.

6. The record of a party's ownership is illustrated in the _____ of title.

7. A _____ is an examination of all the public records to

    determine if defects in title exist.

8. An _____ of title is a summary report of what the title

    search found in the public record.

9. A _____ of title is a statement of opinion of the title's

    status on a certain date.

10. Proof of ownership is evidence that title is _____ .

Key Term Matching

1. The act of placing documents in the public record

2. The legal presumption that information may be obtained through diligent inquiry

3. A type of notice also known as "direct knowledge"

4. The order of rights in time

5. The record of a property's ownership

6. A legal action to remove a cloud on the title and establish legal ownership

7. An examination of all the public records to determine if any defects exist in a property's history of ownership

8. The individual who prepares a summary report of the results of a title search

9. A contract under which a policyholder is protected from losses arising from defects in title

10. A document required by the UCC for a lender to create a lienable interest in personal property

_____ abstractor

_____ actual notice

_____ chain of title

_____ constructive notice

_____ priority

_____ recording

_____ security agreement

_____ suit to quiet title

_____ title insurance

_____ title search

True and False

_____ 1. Any individual who is interested in a particular property may review the public records to learn about the documents, claims and other issues that affect its ownership.

_____ 2. Any written document that affects any estate, right, title or interest in land must be recorded in the county in which the property owner resides.

_____ 3. To be eligible for recording, a document pertaining to real estate must be drawn and executed in accordance with the requirements of the UCC.

_____ 4. Constructive notice means that information about a property is not only available, but that someone has been given access to that information.

_____ 5. A search of the public records will disclose all liens that exist against a property.

_____ 6. The term "chain of title" refers to the record of a property's ownership.

_____ 7. In a typical title search, the chain of title is examined, beginning with the earliest records of ownership and proceeding forward up to the present owner.

_____ 8. A typical abstract of title begins with the original grant and provides a chronological list of recorded instruments up to the present day.

_____ 9. One of the requirements of marketable title is that it could convince a reasonably well-informed and prudent purchaser, acting on business principles and with full knowledge of the significant facts, that the property could be resold or mortgaged at a later time.

_____ 10. A certificate of title is a guarantee of legal ownership.

_____ 11. A standard coverage title insurance policy protects a homeowner against rights of parties in possession and unrecorded liens.

_____ 12. The Torrens system is a legal registration system that is used by a growing number of states.

WRITE YOUR CORRECTIONS BELOW:

_____

_____

_____

_____

_____

_____

_____

_____

_____

_____

_____

_____

Multiple Choice

1. All of the following are acceptable evidence of an owner's title, *EXCEPT* a/an:

   a. abstract of title and attorney's opinion.
   b. recorded deed.
   c. title insurance policy.
   d. certificate of title.

2. Berry Manor is located in Benbo County. It is owned by *T*, who lives in Terrapin County, and subject to a mortgage held by a lender located in Lester County. On August 5, *K* records a lien against the property in the Terrapin County Courthouse; on August 10, *M* records a lien against the property in the Benbo County Courthouse; on August 15, *K* re-records the lien in Lester County. Based on these facts, which lien has priority?

   a. Both liens have equal priority.
   b. *K*'s lien only
   c. *M*'s lien only
   d. Neither lien is properly recorded, so neither has priority.

3. *P* sells Newacre to *Q*. Five years ago, a lien was recorded against Newacre by Rabbit Construction Company. Newacre is in County 12, but the lien was recorded in County 21. When the lien was recorded, *Q* was an active partner in Rabbit Construction. A title search in County 12 disclosed no liens against Newacre. Which of the following is true?

   a. *Q* has constructive notice of the lien but not actual notice, because of the mistake in recording.
   b. *Q* has actual notice of the lien but not constructive notice, because of the mistake in recording.
   c. *Q* has both actual and constructive notice of the lien, because of his association with Rabbit Construction and the recorded lien.
   d. *Q* has no notice of the lien.

4. *N* purchased Blue Acres from *M*. Shortly after closing, *N* discovered that there were serious flaws in the title that made it unlikely that Blue Acres could be resold in the future. What can *N* do now?

   a. Because the title was flawed, *N* can legally void the sale, and *M* must return any consideration.
   b. *N* has no recourse.
   c. Because *M* conveyed unmarketable title, *N* is entitled to a new title report.
   d. Because *N* has accepted the deed, *N*'s only recourse is to sue *M* under any covenants contained in the deed.

5. The person who prepares a certificate of title would be liable for which of the following?

   a. Parties in possession
   b. Negligence in preparing the certificate
   c. Fraudulent past conveyances
   d. Recorded transfers involved forged documents

6. Which of the following would be included in a standard title insurance policy?

   a. Defects discoverable by physical inspection
   b. Unrecorded liens
   c. Forged documents
   d. Easements and restrictive covenants

7. A title insurance policy that protects the interests of a mortgagee is referred to as a/an:

   a. leasehold policy.
   b. lender's policy.
   c. certificate of sale policy.
   d. ALTA policy.

8. The Uniform Commercial Code applies to:

   a. all real property transactions.
   b. sales and leases of commercial property.
   c. real property transactions involving a mortgage loan.
   d. personal property or fixtures used as security for a loan.

Illustration

Figure 13.1 illustrates the complete title record for Lot 27, Block 6 of Springfield Pines Subdivision. Indicate the point at which the chain of title is broken

Figure 13.1   Tracing the Chain of Title

GRANTOR	GRANTEE	BY INSTRUMENT	CONVEYANCE DATE
Ferris-Bumper Builders, Inc	Barton Doyle and Jane Doyle	Warranty Deed	January 19, 1909
Barton Doyle and Jane Doyle	Market Title & Trust Company	Trust Deed	January 20, 1909
Market Title & Trust Company	Barton Doyle and Jane Doyle	Reconveyance Deed	June 10, 1935
Barton Doyle and Jane Doyle	Anton Feldspar	Bargain and Sale Deed	March 7, 1940
Peter Parker and Mary Parker	Lamont Cranston and Gloria Reve	Warranty Deed	November 16, 1958
Lamont Cranston and Gloria Reve	Brookfield Bank and Trust Co.	Mortgage	November 18, 1958
Lamont Cranston and Gloria Reve	Gerald Carlos and Lydi Carlos	Warranty Deed	September 4, 1979
Brookfield Bank and Trust Co.	Lamont Cranston and Gloria Reve	Release	May 2, 1995

14 | Real Estate Financing: Principles

Chapter Summary

1. States that recognize the lender as the owner of mortgaged property are known as _____Title_____ theory states.

2. States that recognize the borrower as the owner of mortgaged property are referred to as _____Lien_____ theory states.

3. States in which the mortgagee is considered the owner of mortgaged property but is required to foreclose to obtain legal title are ___intermediate___ theory states.

4. A ___mortgage___ loan is a financing technique involving only a lender and a borrower.

5. ___Deed of trust___ loans involve a borrower, a lender and a trustee.

6. After a lending institution has received, investigated and approved a loan application, it issues a ___Committment___ to make a mortgage loan.

7. In a mortgage or deed of trust loan, the borrower is required to execute a _____note_____ agreeing to repay the debt.

8. A mortgage or deed of trust is ___recorded___ to give notice to the world of the lender's interest in the property.

9. Full payment of a note by its terms entitles a borrower to a satisfaction, called a

   _____release_____, recorded to clear the lien from the public record.

10. _____Default_____ may result in an acceleration of payments, a

   foreclosure sale and loss of title.

Key Term Matching, Part I

1. The borrower in a mortgage loan

2. The lender in a mortgage loan

3. The act of signing a loan instrument

4. A borrower's personal pledge to repay a debt according to agreed-on terms

5. The pledging of a property as security for payment of a loan without actually surrendering the property itself

6. A financing instrument that conveys bare legal title on behalf of a beneficiary

7. A charge for the use of money

8. The act of charging interest in excess of the maximum legal rate

9. A charge imposed by lenders to adjust for the difference between interest rate and yield

10. The part of a financing agreement that gives the lender the right to declare the entire debt due and payable immediately on default

_10_ acceleration clause

_6_ deed of trust

_9_ discount points

_3_ execute

_5_ hypothecation

_7_ interest

_2_ mortgagee

_1_ mortgagor

_4_ promissory note

_8_ usury

Key Term Matching, Part II

1. The part of a financing agreement that requires the lender to execute a satisfaction or release when the note has been paid in full

2. A provision in a financing agreement that permits the lender to declare the entire debt due immediately in the event the property is sold

3. A device by which one lender agrees to change the priority of its loan relative to another lender

4. A legal procedure in which property pledged as security is sold to satisfy the debt

5. A foreclosure carried out by mutual agreement rather than by legal action

6. A borrower's option of reinstating a defaulted debt prior to the foreclosure sale by paying the amount due

7. A right established by state law that permits a defaulted borrower to recover property within a limited time after a foreclosure sale

8. A procedure for obtaining the unpaid balance of a debt where the foreclosure sale does not generate sufficient funds

2 alienation clause

5 deed in lieu of foreclosure

1 defeasance clause

8 deficiency judgment

6 equitable right of redemption

4 foreclosure

7 statutory right of redemption

3 subordination agreement

True and False

 1. A mortgage is classified as an involuntary lien on real estate.

 2. A mortgage is a two-party financing agreement in which a mortgagee pledges real property to the mortgagor as security for the debt.

__T__ 3. In title theory states, the mortgagor actually gives legal title to the mortgagee, while retaining equitable title.

__T__ 4. When a property is mortgaged, the owner must execute both a promissory note and a security instrument.

__F__ 5. The pledging of property as security for payment of a loan without actually surrendering possession of the property is referred to as ~~subordination.~~ *Hypothecation*

__T__ 6. In a typical deed of trust, the mortgagee is the beneficiary and the borrower is the trustor.

__T__ 7. Usury is defined as the act of charging interest in excess of the maximum legal rate.

__F__ 8. A point is 1 percent of the ~~purchase price of the property being offered as security for the loan.~~ *amt being borrowed*

__F__ 9. A *acceleration* ~~defeasance~~ clause expedites foreclosure by giving a lender the right to declare the entire debt due and payable in the event of a borrower's default.

__T__ 10. By provisions of a defeasance clause in most mortgage documents, the mortgagee is required to execute a satisfaction when the note has been fully paid, returning to the mortgagor all interest in the real estate.

__F__ 11. When a real estate loan secured by a deed of trust has been repaid in full, the beneficiary executes a ~~discharge~~ *release of deed* that releases the property back to the grantor.

__T__ 12. A buyer who purchases real property and assumes the seller's debt becomes personally obligated for the repayment of the entire debt.

__T__ 13. A mortgage or deed of trust must be recorded in the recorder's office of the county in which the real estate is located.

__T__ 14. In states that permit strict foreclosure, no sale of the property takes place.

__T__ 15. The right of a defaulted borrower to redeem his or her real estate within a certain period after the foreclosure sale is known as the statutory right of redemption.

WRITE YOUR CORRECTIONS BELOW:

_____

_____

_____

_____

_____

_____

_____

_____

_____

_____

_____

_____

_____

_____

Multiple Choice

1. *R* defaults on her mortgage, and the lender forecloses. The lender's foreclosure suit is filed on March 15, and the sale is held on May 10. In *R*'s state, a defaulted borrower is permitted to redeem his or her property within 60 days after the date of the sale. If *R* attempts to redeem the property on May 1, which of the following statements is true?

    a. *R* is exercising her statutory right of redemption.
    b. *R* is exercising her equitable right of redemption.
    c. *R*'s attempt to redeem the property is too early; by statute, she must wait until after the sale.
    d. Under these facts, *R* cannot redeem the property.

2. A house is listed for $150,000. *B* buys it for $130,000 and makes a down payment of 20 percent. *B* borrows the balance on a fixed-rate mortgage at 6½ percent. The lender charges four points. If there are no other closing costs involved, how much money should *B* bring to the closing?

    a. $4,160   c. $26,000
    b. $16,000   d. $30,160

3. *P* is a real estate broker. One afternoon, a client calls *P* at home. The client is obviously upset: "My lender just told me that my note and mortgage is a negotiable instrument!" the client says, voice shaking. "What does that mean?" Which of the following would be *P*'s best response?

    a. "That's great! It means the lender is willing to negotiate on the interest rate."
    b. "Oh no! That means the mortgage can't be assumed by the next person you sell to."
    c. "Don't worry! That just means the mortgage can be sold by the lender."
    d. "Uh-oh! That means we have to go back to the sellers and ask them to pay the points."

4. The state of West Oregon is a lien theory state. If *N* purchases Pineacre, and takes out a mortgage loan from *K*, all of the following statements are true, *EXCEPT:*

    a. *N* has retained both legal and equitable title to Pineacre.
    b. if *N* defaults on the loan, *K* must go through a formal foreclosure proceeding to recover the security.
    c. *N* has given legal title to *K*.
    d. *K* has only a lien interest in Pineacre.

5. Where a trust deed is used, the lender is the:

   a. trustee.
   b. beneficiary.
   c. trustor.
   d. maker.

6. The Mortgage Company charges borrowers a 1½ percent loan origination fee. *T* buys a house for $210,000 and pays $50,000 in cash. *T* applies for a mortgage to cover the balance. What will the Mortgage Company charge as a fee if the asking price of the house was $235,000?

   a. $2,400
   b. $3,150
   c. $3,525
   d. $3,750

7. A mortgage document contains the following clause: "In the event of Borrower's default under the terms of this Agreement, Lender may declare the entire unpaid balance of the debt due and payable immediately." This clause is referred to as a/an:

   a. hypothecation clause.
   b. acceleration clause.
   c. defeasance clause.
   d. release clause.

8. This month, *H* made the last payment on a mortgage loan secured by Blackacre. *H*'s lender must exec

   a. release deed.
   b. promissory note.
   c. possessory note.
   d. satisfaction of mortgage.

9. *G* took out a 15-year mortgage on Wetacre in 1992. On April 1, 1997, *G*'s lender discovered that Wetacre lies in a flood hazard area as defined by the National Flood Insurance Reform Act of 1994. The lender informed *G* of the situation on April 15. Based on these facts, which of the following statements is true?

   a. The National Flood Insurance Reform Act of 1994 does not apply to *G*'s property.
   b. *G* has until May 15 to purchase flood insurance.
   c. *G* has until May 30 to purchase flood insurance.
   d. If *G* refuses to purchase flood insurance, the lender must do so, but the lender may not charge the cost of the additional insurance to *G*.

10. *J* purchases Potter's Field from *H* for $45,000 in cash, and assumes *H*'s outstanding mortgage balance of $98,500. The lender executes a release for *H*. *J* fails to make any mortgage payments, and the lender forecloses. At the foreclosure sale, Potter's Field is sold for $75,000. Based on these facts, which of the following statements is true?

   a. *H* is solely liable for $23,500.
   b. *J* is solely liable for $23,500.
   c. *J* and *H* are equally liable for $23,500.
   d. *J* is solely liable for $30,000.

11. All of the following are true of a typical land contract *EXCEPT:*

a. At the end of the loan term, the seller will deliver clear title.
b. The buyer is granted equitable title and possession.
c. The vendee retains legal title during the contract term.
d. In the event of a default, the vendor may retain any money already paid.

12. *B* was the owner of Hasty Manor. When *B* defaulted on his loan, the trustee immediately sold Hasty Manor to recover the debt. The trustee acted under the terms of the security instrument. Based on these facts, which of the following statements is true?

a. The exercise of this power of sale clause is an example of strict foreclosure.
b. The trustee's sale of Hasty Manor was illegal, unless *B*'s state permits such a so-called "friendly foreclosure."
c. The exercise of this power of sale clause is an example of non-judicial foreclosure.
d. *B* could have exercised his statutory right of redemption at any time prior to the trustee's sale of Hasty Acres.

Illustration

*In Figure 14.1, write **Equitable Right of Redemption** and **Statutory Right of Redemption** in the appropriate boxes on the time line.*

Figure 14.1   **Redemption Rights Timeline**

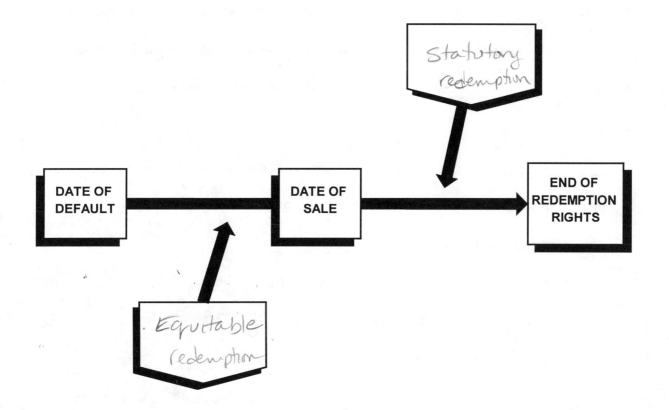

15 Real Estate Financing: Practice

Chapter Summary

1. The federal government affects real estate financing money and interest rates through the discount rate and reserve requirements set by the _Federal Reserve Board_

2. The _Secondary_ market is composed of investors such as insurance companies and pension plans that purchase and hold loans as investments.

3. A _Straight_ loan divides the loan into two amounts, to be paid off separately.

4. _Ammortized_ loans are paid off slowly, over time.

5. In an adjustable-rate loan, interest rates are tied to the movement of an objective economic indicator called an _index_.

6. Mortgage loans are generally classified based on their _loan-to-value (LTV)_ ratio.

7. A note created to make the sale possible is a _purchase-money_ mortgage.

8. Government agencies such as the _FHA_ and _VA_ offer mortgage insurance for qualified loans.

9. _Regulation Z_, promulgated under the _Truth in Lending_ Act, requires that credit institutions inform borrowers of the true cost of obtaining credit.

10. Loan applications can be processed more quickly through the use of an electronic

network known as a (CLO) Computerized Loan system.
Origination

Key Term Matching, Part I

1. A national system of banking districts designed to maintain sound credit conditions and a favorable economic climate

2. The short-term interest rate charged to a bank's largest, most creditworthy customers

3. Lenders who originate loans by making money available to borrowers

4. Thrifts, savings associations and commercial banks

5. Intermediaries who bring borrowers and lenders together

6. Investors who buy and sell loans after funding

7. A quasi-government agency organized as a private, stock-issuing corporation that buys pools of mortgages from lenders in exchange for mortgage-backed securities

8. A wholly governmental agency organized as a nonstock corporation that administers special assistance programs and participates in secondary market activities

9. A type of loan in which the borrower makes periodic interest payments, followed by the payment of the principal in full at the end of the term

10. A loan in which both principal and interest are paid off slowly, over time

_10_ amortized loan

_1_ Federal Reserve

_4_ fiduciary lenders

_7_ FNMA

_8_ GNMA

_5_ mortgage brokers

_3_ primary mortgage market

_2_ prime rate

_6_ secondary mortgage market

_9_ straight loan

Key Term Matching, Part II

1. A form of loan in which the interest rate fluctuates depending on the behavior of an objective economic index

2. A fixed interest-rate mortgage in which payments of principal are increased over the term according to an index or schedule

3. The document that determines the maximum guarantee to which a veteran is entitled

4. A note and mortgage created at the time of purchase

5. A loan that includes both real and personal property

6. A method of financing the purchase of property that temporarily lowers the initial interest rate through the payment of a lump sum of cash to the lender

_1_ adjustable-rate mortgage

_6_ buydown

_3_ certificate of eligibility

_2_ growing-equity mortgage

_5_ package loan

_4_ purchase-money mortgage

True and False

_____ 1. The Federal Reserve System is made up of the lenders who originate loans.

_____ 2. The discount rate is the short-term interest rate charged to a bank's largest, most credit-worthy customers.

_____ 3. Income from a loan is generated by up-front finance charges collected at closings, plus interest collected during the loan term.

_____ 4. The primary mortgage market includes government agencies, insurance companies and mortgage bankers.

_____ 5. The Federal National Mortgage Association ("Fannie Mae) is a privately-owned corporation.

_____ 6. An amortized loan applies each monthly payment first toward the total interest owed over the life of the loan; once the total interest is paid off, each monthly payment is applied to the principal amount.

_____ 7. In an adjustable-rate mortgage, the interest rate is usually based on an objective economic indicator plus an additional premium, called a "margin."

_____ 8. In an adjustable-rate mortgage, the conversion option establishes how often the rate may be changed.

_____ 9. In a 20-year straight loan of $92,500 at 7¾ percent interest, the borrower's final payment will be $93,097.40.

_____ 10. The "value" portion of a property's LTV is the higher of the sale price or the appraised value.

_____ 11. The FHA is not a mortgage lender.

_____ 12. Unlike the FHA, the VA makes purchase-money loans to qualified individuals.

_____ 13. A wraparound loan covers more than one parcel or lot, and is usually used to finance subdivision developments.

_____ 14. In an open-end loan, the interest rate on the initial amount borrowed is fixed, but the rate on future advances is linked to future market rates.

_____ 15. Under Regulation Z, consumers must be fully informed of all finance charges, and the true interest rate, prior to the completion of a transaction.

_____ 16. Under the Equal Credit Opportunity Act, a residential purchase-money borrower has three days in which to rescind a transaction simply by notifying the lender of his or her intent to rescind.

_____ 17. Under the Community Reinvestment Act, the findings of the government agency review of an institution's reinvestment activities are strictly confidential.

_____ 18. A computerized loan origination system allows a real estate broker to select a lender and apply for a loan on a buyer's behalf.

WRITE YOUR CORRECTIONS BELOW:

Multiple Choice

1. *K*'s monthly mortgage payment is $520. The interest rate on the loan is 10 percent, and the outstanding balance is $43,500. When *K* makes this month's payment, what amount of the total payment will be applied to interest, and what amount to principal?

   a. $362.50 interest; 157.50 principal
   b. $435.00 interest; $85.00 principal
   c. $520.00 interest; $0 principal
   d. $85.00 interest; $435.00 principal

2. All of the following are true regarding the Federal Reserve System, *EXCEPT:*

   a. all federally chartered banks must join the Federal Reserve System and purchase stock in its district reserve banks.
   b. the Federal Reserve requires that member banks set aside assets as reserve funds for use exclusively as mortgage loans.
   c. by increasing or decreasing reserve requirements, the Federal Reserve controls the amount of money available for mortgage loans.
   d. member banks are permitted to borrow money from the reserve banks to expand their local banking operations.

3. All of the following are lenders in the primary mortgage market, *EXCEPT:*

   a. endowment funds.
   b. mortgage brokers.
   c. insurance companies.
   d. credit unions.

4. If a buyer obtains a loan for $13,500, and the interest rate is 7½ percent, what is the amount of semiannual interest payable?

   a. $457.14   c. $596.55
   b. $506.25   d. $602.62

5. A house had a sales price of $80,000. The buyer obtained a loan for $72,000. If the lender charges three points, what will the buyer pay?

   a. $1,980   c. $2,420
   b. $2,160   d. $2,610

6. Last month, *M*'s total mortgage payment included $412.50 in interest on a loan with an outstanding balance of $60,000. What is *M*'s annual rate of interest?

   a. 7½ percent   c. 8¼ percent
   b. 7¾ percent   d. 8½ percent

To answer the following question, refer to Table 15.1 in Modern Real Estate Practice, *14th Edition.*

7. T has a 25-year mortgage loan for $90,000. The interest rate on the loan is 6½ percent. What is T's monthly principal and interest payment?

    a. $533.33
    b. $600.30
    c. $607.50
    d. $614.70

8. Under the terms of *B*'s adjustable-rate mortgage, the interest rate *B* must pay is (1) the U.S. Treasury bill rate as of June 1 of each year, not to exceed 8.95 percent for any period; plus (2) 1.5 percent. What is the term used to describe (2)?

    a. rate cap
    b. index
    c. margin
    d. payment cap

9. *G* bought a charming cottage overlooking the ocean. The asking price for the cottage was $85,000; *G* offered $83,550 and the seller accepted. The appraised value of the cottage is $82,000. *G* plans to pay $15,000 in cash and take out a mortgage for the remainder. What is the LTV for this property?

    a. 80 percent
    b. 82 percent
    c. 84 percent
    d. 89 percent

10. A borrower took out an FHA-insured loan on a single-family home on August 1, 1995. If the borrower wishes to prepay the loan, which of the following statements is true?

    a. The borrower must give the lender 30 days' written notice of his or her intent to prepay and may be charged a penalty of one month's interest.
    b. If the borrower fails to give the lender 30 days written notice of his or her intent to prepay, the lender has the option of charging a penalty of up to 30 days' interest.
    c. No written notice is required, but lenders are permitted to charge a reasonable prepayment penalty.
    d. No written notice is required and there is no prepayment penalty.

11. *P* is buying Hilltop House from *R*. *R* bought Hilltop House on December 14, 1989, with an FHA loan, and has lived there ever since. Because of its favorable terms, *P* would like to assume *R*'s mortgage. Is this possible?

    a. Yes; there are no restrictions on the assumption of this mortgage.
    b. Yes, but P will have to go through the complete buyer qualification process.
    c. Yes, but P will have to undergo a creditworthiness review.
    d. No; this FHA loan is unassumable.

12. In 1967, *R* served for six months on active duty in Vietnam. After winning a medal for bravery and being honorably discharged, *R* went back to college, received a degree in engineering, and went to work for a large construction company. In 1993, *R* was killed in a tragic skiing accident. *R*'s widow wishes to use *R*'s life insurance money to make a down payment on a condominium, and believes she is entitled to a VA-guaranteed loan. Is she correct?

    a. Yes; the unremarried spouse of a qualified veteran is entitled to a VA-guaranteed loan.
    b. Yes; whether or not she remarries, *R*'s widow is entitled to the same VA benefits as *R* was during his life.
    c. No; *R*'s death was not service-related.
    d. No; *R* did not meet the time-in-service criteria for qualified veterans.

13. Which of the following makes direct loans to qualified borrowers?

    a. VA   c. Fannie Mae
    b. FSA   d. FHA

14. *K* is purchasing a fully furnished condominium unit. In this situation, *K* would be most likely to use a:

    a. package loan.
    b. blanket loan.
    c. wraparound loan.
    d. buydown.

15. The Equal Credit Opportunity Act prohibits lenders from discriminating against credit applicants on the basis of all of the following factors, *EXCEPT:*

    a. religion.
    b. past credit history.
    c. income from public assistance.
    d. marital status.

16. *G*, a real estate broker, has a CLO terminal in her office. Because there are more than a dozen lending institutions in the city, *G* has found that the CLO greatly streamlines the application process for her clients. *G* sits down at the terminal with *B*, a home buyer, and the following events take place:

    (1) *G* explains that there is a fee for using the terminal of one-half point, based on the loan amount, and that *B* may choose to finance the fee; (2) *G* explains the different kinds of services offered by the two local lenders who pay *G* a monthly "screen fee," to be included on the CLO system; and (3) *G* helps *B* answer the on-screen qualification questions.

    Which of these events is an improper use of a CLO system?

    a. 1 only   c. 2 and 3
    b. 2 only   d. 1 and 3

Illustration

Carlos and Wendy have just purchased a house for $92,000. They are looking for a 30-year loan and have been quoted an interest rate of 8 percent. Now they are trying to decide if they should obtain an 80 percent conventional loan, a 90 percent conventional loan or an FHA-insured loan or use Wendy's VA eligibility to obtain a VA-guaranteed loan. To help Carlos and Wendy make a decision, fill in the table in Figure 15.1. (Use the mortgage rate factor of $7.34/$1,000 of loan amount to determine the principal and interest per month; ignore the effect of closing costs.)

Figure 15.1

TYPE OF LOAN	PURCHASE PRICE	MAXIMUM LOAN	DOWN PAYMENT	P&I PER MONTH
80% CONVENTIONAL	$92,000			
90% CONVENTIONAL	$92,000			
FHA	$92,000			
VA	$92,000			

16 Leases

Chapter Summary

1. A _____lease_____ is an agreement that grants one person the right to use another's property in return for consideration.

2. A leasehold estate for a specific period creates an __estate__ for __years__.

3. A leasehold that runs for an indefinite period creates an estate _from period to period._

4. An estate __at will__ runs as long as the landlord permits.

5. An estate __at sufferance__ is possession without the landlord's consent.

6. A leasehold estate is classified as __personal__ property.

7. A lease is a type of __contract__.

8. A lease may be __terminated__ by the expiration of the lease period, the mutual agreement of the parties or a breach by either landlord or tenant.

9. If leased premises become uninhabitable due to the landlord's negligence, the tenant may have the remedy of __constructive eviction__

10. The __Americans w/ Disabilitie__ Act provides for access to goods and services by people with disabilities.

Key Term Matching

1. A contract between a real estate owner and a tenant

2. A landlord's right to possession of the premises after the expiration of the lease term

3. A tenant's right to possess real estate for the term of a lease

4. A leasehold estate that continues for a definite period

5. The estate created when a landlord and tenant enter into an agreement without a specific expiration date

6. A leasehold estate that gives the tenant the right to possess property with the landlord's consent for an uncertain term

7. The leasehold estate created when a tenant who was in lawful possession of real property continues in possession without the landlord's consent

8. A tenant's act of transferring all his or her leasehold interests to another person

9. The transfer of less than all of a tenant's interests

10. A lessee's privilege of renewing a lease

11. The process by which a landlord regains possession of leased premises following a tenant's breach

12. The action by which a tenant may properly abandon premises that have become unusable due to the landlord's conscious neglect

---

_11_ actual eviction

_8_ assignment

_12_ constructive eviction

_1_ lease

_3_ leasehold

_10_ option

_5_ periodic tenancy

_2_ reversionary right

_9_ sublease

_7_ tenancy at sufferance

_6_ tenancy at will

_4_ tenancy for years

True and False

_____ 1. In a lease agreement, the landlord is the lessee and the tenant is the lessor.

_____ 2. Unlike a freehold estate, a leasehold estate is considered personal property.

_____ 3. Although an extension of a tenancy for years requires a new contract, the lease may be terminated prior to the expiration date by either party at any time.

_____ 4. Periodic tenancies are characterized by continuity because they are automatically renewable.

_____ 5. The main difference between a tenancy at will and a tenancy at sufferance is the landlord's consent.

_____ 6. The elements of a valid lease are (1) offer and acceptance, (2) capacity of the parties, (3) consideration, and (4) legal objective.

_____ 7. The covenant of quiet enjoyment is a guarantee by the landlord that the tenant is entitled to possession of the premises without interference from the landlord.

_____ 8. A tenant who is leasing only a part of a building is not required to continue paying rent if the leased premises are destroyed.

_____ 9. When a tenant transfers all of his or her leasehold interests to another person, he or she has assigned the lease.

_____10. Under a net lease agreement, the landlord pays all the operating expenses of the property, while the tenant pays only a fixed rental.

_____11. Ground leases are generally long-term net leases.

_____12. Except in the case of a tenancy at will or a lease from the owner of a life estate, the death of one of the parties does not terminate the lease.

_____13. To be entitled to constructive eviction, the tenant must show only that the premises have become unusable for the purpose stated in the lease.

_____14. The Fair Housing Amendments Act of 1988 requires that, in leased housing, the same criteria must be applied to tenants with children as are applied to adults.

Write your corrections below:

_____

_____

_____

_____

_____

_____

_____

_____

_____

_____

_____

_____

Multiple Choice

1. *N* rents an apartment from *R* under a one-year written lease. The expiration date of the lease is May 1. How much notice must *R* give *N* to recover possession on May 1?

   a. 30 days
   b. 60 days
   c. One week
   d. No notice is required

2. In 1992, *M* rented Brownacre to *N*. The agreement stated only that *N* agreed to pay *M* $500 per month. What type of tenancy does *N* have?

   a. Holdover   c. For years
   b. At sufferance   d. Periodic

3. *S* rents an apartment under a two-year written lease from *C*. Three months after signing the lease, *S* is transferred to another country for a year. During this period, *S* leases the apartment to *J*. *J* mails monthly rent checks to *S*, who continues making monthly rental payments to *C*. In this situation, *J* has a:

   a. lease.
   b. tenancy at will.
   c. sublease.
   d. periodic tenancy.

4. *F* lives in an apartment building owned by *H*. On a Monday during a particularly hot August, vandals break into the building and destroy the central air-conditioning system. *F*'s apartment becomes uncomfortably warm. On Tuesday, *F* sues *H* for constructive eviction. Under these facts, will *F* win?

   a. Yes, if *F*'s lease promises that the apartment will be air conditioned.
   b. Yes; to claim constructive eviction, it is not necessary that the condition be the result of the landlord's personal actions.
   c. No; to claim constructive eviction, the tenant must prove that the premises are uninhabitable.
   d. No; the premises are not unusable, the condition was not due to *H*'s conscious neglect and *F* has not abandoned the apartment.

5. *V* is a tenant in Bountiful Towers under a one-year lease signed in August.
   Rent payments are due on the 15th of
   each month. On December 12, Bountiful Towers is sold to a new owner.
   On March 14, the building burns to
   the ground. Which of the following
   statements accurately describes *V*'s
   obligations?

   a. *V* is not required to continue pay-
      ing rent after March 14, because
      the premises have been destroyed.
   b. *V* is not required to continue pay-
      ing rent after December 12, be-
      cause the sale voids the preexist-
      ing lease.
   c. *V* is required to continue paying
      rent for the full lease term, be-
      cause a tenancy for years cannot
      be terminated by the destruction
      of the premises.
   d. *V* is required to continue paying
      rent, but the residential lease is
      converted by law into a ground
      lease.

6. *J* signs a lease to rent an apartment.
   J's lease runs from October 1 until
   November 1 of the following year. *K*
   signs a one-year lease to rent an
   apartment in a new highrise building
   that will be ready for occupancy in 15
   months. Which of these leases must
   be in writing to satisfy the statute of
   frauds?

   a. *J*'s only
   b. *K*'s only
   c. Both *J*'s and *K*'s
   d. Neither *J*'s nor *K*'s

7. A tenant signed a one-year lease with
   a landlord on April 10, 1997. On
   March 1, 1998, the landlord asked the
   tenant whether the lease would be re-
   newed. The tenant did not respond,
   but was still in the apartment on April
   11, 1998. What can the landlord do?

   a. The landlord must initiate eviction
      proceedings within the first one-
      month rental period.
   b. The landlord cannot evict the ten-
      ant; because the tenant remained
      in possession of the premises, the
      lease has been automatically re-
      newed for an additional year.
   c. If the landlord accepts a rent
      check, the tenant is entitled to a
      renewal of the one-year lease.
   d. The landlord may either evict the
      holdover tenant or accept a rent
      check, creating a periodic
      tenancy.

8. If a tenant remains in possession of
   leased property after the expiration
   of the lease term, without paying
   rent and without the landlord's consent, what is his or her status?

   a. Tenant at will
   b. Tenant at sufferance
   c. Periodic tenant
   d. Freehold tenant

9. *J* wanted to rent an apartment from *K*. Because of a physical disability, it would be necessary for *J* to have all the doorknobs and light switches in the unit lowered to a height of 12 inches from the floor. This would require the installation of new doors and locks, custom-made appliances and the complete rewiring of both *J*'s unit and several neighboring apartments. In addition, the floors in *J*'s unit would have to be reinforced by installing steel beams and posts in the apartment beneath and in the basement. Based on these facts, which of the following statements is true?

a. The Fair Housing Act requires that *K* make the accommodation for *J* at *K*'s expense; no additional rent may be charged for *J*'s modified unit.
b. If the modifications demanded by *J* are not reasonable, *K* is not legally required to permit them.
c. Regardless of the nature of the modifications, *J*'s access right is protected by the Americans with Disabilities Act, and *K* is legally obligated to permit the modifications to be made at *J*'s expense.
d. Because the proposed modifications would interfere with a future tenant's use of the premises, *K* may refuse to permit them.

10. *G* rented a house from *R*. During the lease term, *G* had to move out of state. *G* assigned the lease to *P*, who failed to make any rental payments. In this situation, which of the following statements is true?

a. *G* has no obligation to *R*, because the lease was assigned, not sublet.
b. *P* has no obligation to *R*, because *P*'s lease agreement is with *G*.
c. *G* is still liable to *R* for the outstanding rent, unless *R* released *G* when the lease was assigned to *P*.
d. *G* is still liable to *R*, because *G*'s arrangement with *P* as described is a sublease, not an assignment.

11. *N* operates a small store in a shopping center. Under the terms of the lease, the landlord pays all operating expenses. *N* pays a base rent of $1,000 per month, plus 15 percent of monthly gross profits over $10,000. *N* has a:

a. gross lease.
b. percentage lease.
c. net lease.
d. variable lease.

12. When a landowner leases unimproved land to a tenant, who agrees to erect a building on the land, the lease is usually referred to as a/an:

a. lease purchase.
b. gross lease.
c. ground lease.
d. improvement lease.

Illustration

Figure 16.1 shows part of the Happy Shoppers Mall in the exclusive suburban community of West Flightpath. Based on the information given below, write the type of lease and current month's rental beneath each store.

1. *Acrylic Acres pays a base rent of $1,500 per month and 15 percent of property charges, limited to utilities and taxes. Blue Buttons Boutique pays a base rent of $2,000 per month and no property charges. Custom Custards pays a base rent of $1,850 per month and no property charges, but pays 12 percent of its monthly gross sales over $4,000 to the landlord.*

2. *Acrylic Acres earned $10,000 in gross profits and netted $4,850. Blue Buttons Boutique grossed $6,500 and earned a net profit of $3,000. Custom Custards had a gross income of $9,542, with profits after expenses of $7,370 for the month.*

3. *This month, the Happy Shoppers Mall had to pay $6,790 in utility bills and $495 in regular repairs and maintenance. The month's prorated share of local property taxes was $2,560, and the prorated insurance fee was $900.*

Figure 16.1   **Types of Commercial Leases**

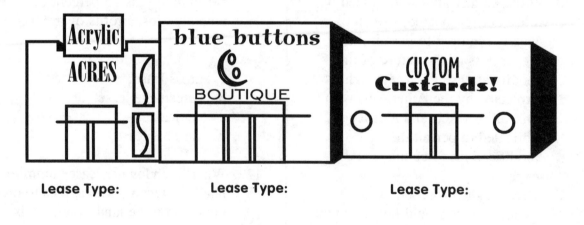

Lease Type: Lease Type: Lease Type:

Rent: Rent: Rent:

215

17 Property Management

Chapter Summary

1. Property management is a specialized professional service offered to owners of

   _____ -producing properties.

2. The manager, as _____ of the owner, administers and

   maintains the property.

3. A _____ establishes the relationship between the owner

   and manager by defining the manager's responsibilities.

4. One of a manager's primary responsibilities is to collect _____.

5. _____ includes safeguarding the physical integrity of the

   property and performing routine cleaning and repairs.

6. The manager is expected to secure adequate _____

   coverage for the premises.

7. _____ insurance covers the property and fixtures against

   catastrophes.

8. _____ insurance provides coverage against losses such as

   theft, vandalism and destruction of machinery.

9. The property manager should secure _____ insurance to insure the owner against claims made by people injured on the premises.

10. _____ policies cover the claims of employees injured while on the job.

Key Term Matching

1. The document that creates the agency relationship between an owner and property manager

2. The process of determining both the initial and operating costs of equipment over its expected life

3. Performance of regularly scheduled activities such as painting and servicing appliances and systems

4. Major alterations to a building's interior to meet a tenant's particular needs

5. Evaluating and preparing for potential liabilities

6. An owner's protection against financial losses due to an employee's criminal acts

7. Insurance policies that offer a package of standard coverages

8. Insurance policies that provide coverage against theft, burglary and vandalism

9. Insurance that covers the results of a disaster

10. An investigation to determine the need for insurance and types of insurance required

_____audit

_____casualty

_____consequential loss

_____life cycle costing

_____management agreement

_____multiperil

_____preventive maintenance

_____risk management

_____surety bond

_____tenant improvements

True and False

_____ 1. A property manager has three principal responsibilities: financial management, physical management and administrative management.

_____ 2. The management agreement creates a special agency relationship between an owner and the property manager.

_____ 3. Unlike real estate brokers' commissions, property management fees may be standardized by local associations.

_____ 4. Rental rates are influenced primarily by supply and demand.

_____ 5. If the vacancy rate in a building is high, the rent is probably too high.

_____ 6. The manager of a residential building should carefully consider a prospective tenant's compatibility with existing tenants.

_____ 7. A high tenant turnover rate results in higher profits for the owner.

_____ 8. The four types of maintenance necessary to keep a property in good condition are preventive, corrective, construction and routine.

_____ 9. Corrective maintenance helps prevent problems and expenses before they arise.

_____ 10. Tenant improvements are major alterations to the interior of commercial or industrial property, usually performed by the tenant prior to moving in.

_____ 11. Under Title I of the ADA, all existing barriers must be removed from both residential and commercial properties.

_____ 12. The ADA requirements for new construction are stricter than those for existing buildings.

_____ 13. The four alternative risk management techniques are transfer, control, avoid and retain.

_____ 14. In a commercial property, the risk of a shopper suffering a slip-and-fall injury would be covered by casualty insurance.

_____15. A building is insured for what it would cost to rebuild it in a depreciated value policy.

WRITE YOUR CORRECTIONS BELOW:

_____

_____

_____

_____

_____

_____

_____

_____

_____

_____

_____

_____

_____

Multiple Choice

1. A property manager's first responsibility to the owner should be to:

   a. keep the building's occupancy rate at 100 percent.
   b. report all day-to-day financial and operating decisions to the owner on a regular basis.
   c. realize the highest profit possible consistent with the owner's instructions.
   d. ensure that the rental rates are below market average.

2. The property manager's relationship with the owner is most similar to that of a/an:

   a. partner in a partnership.
   b. employee in a store.
   c. stockholder in a corporation.
   d. real estate agent.

3. All of the following should be included in a written management agreement, *EXCEPT* a/an:

   a. list of the manager's duties and responsibilities.
   b. statement of the owner's purpose.
   c. statement identifying the manager's creditors.
   d. allocation of costs.

4. If apartment 3B rents for $750 per month and the manager receives a 12 percent commission on all new tenants, how much will the manager receive when he or she rents 3B, assuming that this commission is calculated in the usual way?

   a. $90   c. $1,080
   b. $750   d. $1,800

5. What would be the annual rent per square foot for a 30- by 40-foot property that rents for $2,950 per month?

   a. $1.20   c. $24.65
   b. $2.46   d. $29.50

6. A high vacancy rate most likely indicates:

   a. rental rates are too low.
   b. the property is desirable.
   c. building management is effective and responsive.
   d. tenant dissatisfaction.

7. Which of the following is an example of corrective maintenance?

   a. Seasonal servicing of appliances
   b. Picking up litter in common areas
   c. Repairing a hot water heater
   d. Moving a partition wall to make a larger office space

8. The Americans with Disabilities Act applies to:

   a. commercial and residential properties and all employers.
   b. commercial properties and employers of persons with disabilities.
   c. commercial properties and employers of at least 15 employees.
   d. new residential construction and employers of at least 15 people.

9. Under the ADA, existing barriers must be removed:

   a. in all public buildings by the end of 1997.
   b. only on request from a person with a disability.
   c. when achievable in a "reasonably inexpensive manner."
   d. when removal may be accomplished in a "readily achievable manner."

10. A company was moving from one part of the city to another. During the move, a computer worth more than $750,000 was accidentally dropped into the river. Fortunately, the company was insured under several policies. The policy that would most likely cover the computer during the move from one facility to another is a:

   a. consequential loss, use and occupancy policy.
   b. casualty policy.
   c. contents and personal property policy.
   d. liability policy.

Illustration

*In Figure 17.1, identify each maintenance job as **Preventive**, **Corrective**, **Routine** or **Construction**. Indicate on the floor plan the approximate location of each problem.*

Figure 17.1   Building Maintenance and Property Management

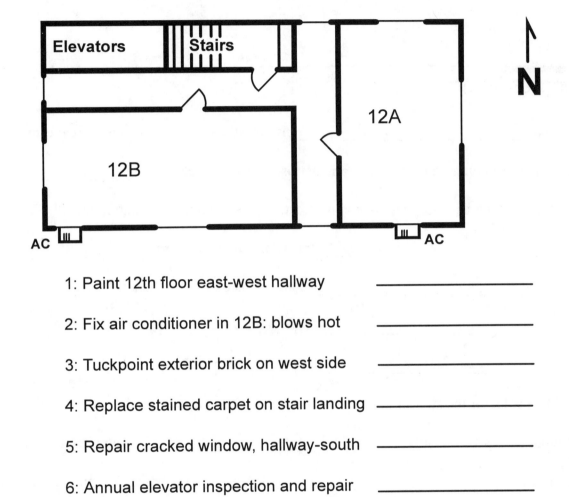

1: Paint 12th floor east-west hallway   _____

2: Fix air conditioner in 12B: blows hot   _____

3: Tuckpoint exterior brick on west side   _____

4: Replace stained carpet on stair landing   _____

5: Repair cracked window, hallway-south   _____

6: Annual elevator inspection and repair   _____

7: Reverse 12A entry door to open in; widen doorway and replace door to accommodate tenant in wheelchair   _____

18 Real Estate Appraisal

Chapter Summary

1. An _____appraisal_____ is an estimation of the value of real estate.

2. The most common objective of an appraisal is to estimate _____market value_____.

3. Highest and best use, supply and demand, regression and contribution are all

   _____economic_____ principles basic to appraisal.

4. _____Value_____ is an estimate of future benefits.

5. _____Cost_____ represents a measure of past expenditures.

6. _____Price_____ reflects the actual amount paid for a property.

7. The value of the subject property is compared with values of other, similar properties

   that have sold recently in the _____sales comparison_____ approach.

8. In the _____cost_____ approach, an appraiser calculates the cost of

   building a similar structure on a similar site.

9. The _____income_____ approach is based on the relationship between

   the rate of return that an investor requires and the net revenue that a property produces.

10. An informal version of the income approach, the _____gross rent multiplier_____, may

    be used to estimate the value of single-family residential properties that could be rented.

11. For commercial and industrial properties, value may be estimated based on annual

income from all sources with the ___Gross income multiplier___

12. In the process of ___reconciliation___, the appraiser weighs each

approach to valuation objectively, to arrive at the most supportable estimate of value.

Key Term Matching, Part I

1. An estimate or opinion of value, based on supportable evidence and approved methods

2. An independent professional who is trained to provide an unbiased estimate of value

3. The relative ease with which ownership rights are conveyed from one person to another

4. The most probable price that a property should bring in a fair sale

5. The principle that value is created by the expectation that certain events will occur in the future

6. The principle that no physical or economic condition remains constant

7. The principle that value is created when a property is in harmony with its surroundings

8. The principle that the value of any part of a property is measured by its effect on the value of the whole property

9. The most profitable single use to which property may be put

10. The process of merging two separately owned lots under one owner

___5___ anticipation

___1___ appraisal

___2___ appraiser

___10___ assemblage

___6___ change

___7___ conformity

___8___ contribution

___9___ highest and best use

___4___ market value

___3___ transferability

Key Term Matching, Part II

1. The principle that merging or consolidating adjacent lots into a single one will produce a higher total value than the sum of the two sites valued separately

2. The principle that the worth of a better-quality property is adversely affected by the presence of a lesser-quality property

3. The principle that the worth of a lesser-quality property is enhanced by the presence of a better-quality property

4. The principle that the maximum value of a property tends to be set by how much it would cost to purchase an equally desirable property

5. The economic principle that the value of a property depends on the number of similar properties available in the marketplace

6. The approach that estimates value by comparing the subject property with recently sold similar properties

7. An estimate of value by determining the value of the land as if it were vacant, adding the current cost of constructing improvements, and deducting accrued depreciation

8. The cost of constructing an exact duplicate of the subject property at current prices

9. The current price of constructing a property similar to the subject property

10. A loss in value due to any cause

11. The period during which a property is expected to remain useful for its original intended purpose

12. An estimate of value based on the present worth of the rights to future income

___7___ cost approach

___10___ depreciation

___11___ economic life

___12___ income approach

___1___ plottage

___3___ progression

___2___ regression

___9___ replacement cost

___8___ reproduction cost

___6___ sales comparison

___4___ substitution

___5___ supply and demand

True and False

_____ 1. Title XI of FIRREA requires that all residential property be appraised by a federally licensed or certified appraiser.

_____ 2. A competitive market analysis should never be represented as an appraisal.

_____ 3. The market value of a property is what it actually sells for in an open market transaction.

_____ 4. Cost and market value are the same.

_____ 5. The value of a property may be affected by events that have not actually occurred.

_____ 6. The law of diminishing returns applies when, no matter how much money is spent on a property, its value will not keep pace with the expenditures.

_____ 7. According to the economic principle of plottage, combining two adjacent lots into a larger one will produce a higher total land value than the sum of the value of the two sites if owned separately.

_____ 8. The economic principle of contribution holds that the maximum value of a property tends to be set by the cost of purchasing a similarly desirable property.

_____ 9. In the sales comparison approach to value, a feature that is present in the subject property but not present in a comparable property is subtracted from the sale price of the comparable.

_____ 10. The square-foot method and the unit-in-place method are both characteristic of the cost approach to value.

_____ 11. Depreciation may be curable or incurable, depending on whether the expense required contributes to the property's value.

_____ 12. External obsolescence is always incurable.

_____ 13. The income approach to value is based on the future value of the rights to present income.

_____ 14. A GRM or GIM is often used as a substitute for an income capitalization analysis.

_____15. Reconciliation involves averaging the results derived from the three approaches to value.

WRITE YOUR CORRECTIONS BELOW:

_____

_____

_____

_____

_____

_____

_____

_____

_____

_____

_____

_____

Multiple Choice

1. All of the following properties would have to be appraised by a state licensed or certified appraiser as required by FIRREA, assuming that all of the transactions are federally-related, *EXCEPT* a:

   a. commercial property valued at $2.5 million.
   b. condominium unit with a sales price of $67,850.
   c. residential property valued at $262,500.
   d. commercial property valued over $1 million in a refinance.

2. A property is listed for sale at $235,000. A buyer's offer of $220,000 is rejected by the seller. Six months later, the seller reduces the price to $225,000. Another buyer offers $210,000 and the seller accepts. The property is subsequently appraised at $215,000. Which of these figures accurately represents the property's market value?

   a. $210,000   c. $225,000
   b. $215,000   d. $235,000

3. The principle that maximum value is realized when land use is in harmony with surrounding standards is:

   a. contribution.
   b. conformity.
   c. highest and best use.
   d. competition.

4. K plans to build a large house in a neighborhood of smaller homes, so K purchases three neighboring lots from their three owners. What is the term for K's activity?

   a. Substitution   c. Progression
   b. Plottage   d. Assemblage

5. L buys a small house in a desirable neighborhood of large Victorian homes and pays $190,000. L's friend M buys a nearly identical house in a neighborhood of similar homes and pays $100,000. What economic principle best describes the reason why L paid more than M?

   a. Plottage   c. Regression
   b. Substitution   d. Progression

6. If Blandacre were vacant, undeveloped land it would be worth about $40,000. To build Blandacre Manor and its various improvements today would cost approximately $200,000. As it currently exists, Blandacre Manor's physical deterioration is worth about $30,000. If an appraiser were to apply the cost approach, what would be Blandacre's value?

   a. $130,000   c. $220,000
   b. $210,000   d. $240,000

7. In which approach to value are the square-foot method, the unit-in-place method and the quantity-survey method used?

   a. Sales comparison approach
   b. Cost approach
   c. Income approach
   d. Reconciliation approach

8. The Ghastlie Theatre Building is considered a premier example of external ornamentation. Carved marble gargoyles and granite baskets of glazed terra cotta fruit decorate the entire front of the building. Unfortunately, increased automobile traffic in the downtown area has resulted in air pollution that has dissolved much of the intricate detail work. The cost of restoring the front of the building is roughly five times the building's present value. These facts describe which of the following?

   a. Curable external obsolescence
   b. Incurable functional obsolescence
   c. Incurable physical deterioration
   d. Curable external deterioration

9. The land on which Crumbling Manor was built is worth $50,000. The Manor was constructed in 1975 at a cost of $265,000, and is expected to last 50 years. Using the straight-line method, determine how much Crumbling Manor has depreciated by 1997.

   a. $28,600   c. $116,600
   b. $94,600   d. $145,200

10. All of the following formulas are correct, *EXCEPT:*

    a. Income ÷ Value = Rate.
    b. Income ÷ Rate = Value.
    c. Value ÷ Rate = Income.
    d. Value x Rate = Income.

11. What is the GRM for a three-unit apartment building with a selling price of $362,500 if the monthly rent for each apartment is $900?

    a. 1.087   c. 134.3
    b. 108.8   d. 402.8

12. Which of the following approaches is given the greatest weight in reconciling the appraised value of a two-bedroom, owner-occupied home?

    a. Income approach
    b. Sales comparison approach
    c. Cost approach
    d. Market value approach

Illustration

There are five homes on the 1200 block of Pennytree Lane, pictured in Figure 18.1. Complete the figure by solving the various appraisal problems presented.

Figure 18.1   **Appraisal Problems on Pennytree Lane**

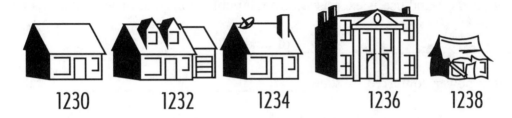

1230   1232   1234   1236   1238

1. 1230 Pennytree Lane was just sold. Which house is the best comparable property? _____

2. The principle of regression is best illustrated by which properties? _____

3. The principle of progression is best illustrated by which properties? _____

4. Pennytree Lane is near an increasingly fashionable and upscale part of town. Incomes in the area are rising rapidly. If 1236 is a newly-constructed home, it is an example of which principle of value? _____

5. When 1232 added a garage, what likely happened to the values of 1230 and 1234? _____

6. 1236 violates which principle of value? _____

7. When 1234 added a satellite dish, which principle of value describes its effect? _____

KEY
219

19 Land-Use Controls and Property Development

Chapter Summary

1. The control of land use is exercised through public controls, private controls and _____ of land.

2. Through power conferred by state _____, local governments exercise public controls based on the state's _____ to protect the public health, safety and welfare.

3. _____ set development goals for the community.

4. _____ carry out the provisions of the plan and control the use of land and structures within designated land-use districts.

5. _____ specify standards for construction, plumbing, sewers, electrical wiring and equipment.

6. Benefits such as parks, highways and schools may be provided for by direct _____ ownership of land.

7. A _____ buys undeveloped acreage, divides it into smaller parcels and then develops or sells it.

8. A _____ builds homes on unimproved parcels and sells

them either through his or her own sales organization or through a real estate broker.

9. Land development must comply with the _____ adopted by

local governments.

10. The process of _____ includes dividing land into lots and

blocks, providing utility easements and laying out street patterns and widths.

11. A subdivider must generally record a completed and approved _____

of subdivision in the county in which the property is located.

12. _____ housing units can dramatically increase the amount

of open and recreational space within a development.

13. Private land-use controls are exercised by owners through deed_____

and restrictive _____ .

14. Federal law requires developers engaged in certain _____

land sales or leases to register the details of the property with HUD.

Key Term Matching, Part I

1. The device by which local governments establish development goals

2. Another term for a community's proposed framework for controlling growth and development

3. Local laws that implement a comprehensive plan and regulate the control of land and structures within districts

4. The legal means by which states confer zoning powers on local governments

5. Areas such as parks used to screen residential from nonresidential areas

6. A special type of zoning used to control density by imposing restrictions such as setbacks or limiting new construction

7. The seizure of land through the government's power of eminent domain or condemnation

8. A lot or improvement that is not in harmony with current zoning because it existed prior to the enactment or amendment of the zoning

9. The device by which a day-care center might be permitted to operate in a residential neighborhood

10. The device by which a landowner may use his or her property in a manner that is otherwise strictly prohibited by the existing zoning ordinances

_____ buffer zones

_____ bulk zoning

_____ comprehensive plan

_____ conditional-use permit

_____ enabling acts

_____ master plan

_____ nonconforming use

_____ taking

_____ variance

_____ zoning ordinances

Key Term Matching, Part II

1. The device by which municipal officials are alerted to new construction and alterations

2. A person who buys undeveloped acreage and divides it into smaller lots for sale to others

3. An individual who constructs improvements and sells them

4. A detailed map that illustrates the geographic boundaries of individual lots

5. Ordinances that restrict the average maximum number of houses per acre

6. Standards for building style, setbacks and use that are included in a deed for property in a subdivision

7. Ordinances that specify construction and safety standards for construction

_____ building codes

_____ building permit

_____ density zoning

_____ developer

_____ plat

_____ restrictive covenants

_____ subdivider

True and False

_____ 1. Zoning ordinances create the broad, general framework for a community; the comprehensive plan defines the details and implements the ordinances.

_____ 2. Bulk zoning is used to ensure that certain types of uses are incorporated into developments.

_____ 3. Property owners are protected against the unreasonable or arbitrary taking of their land by the seizure clause of the Fifteenth Amendment to the United States Constitution.

_____ 4. The government's payment to a landowner for seizure of his or her property is referred to as "just compensation."

_____ 5. A conditional use permit allows a landowner to use his or her property in a manner that is otherwise strictly prohibited by the existing zoning.

_____ 6. A property owner who wants to build a structure or alter or repair an existing building usually must first obtain a zoning permit.

_____ 7. A subdivider is a person who buys undeveloped acreage and divides it into smaller lots for sale to individuals or developers.

_____ 8. Zoning is a state and local issue; there is no national zoning ordinance.

_____ 9. A detailed map that illustrates the geographic boundaries of individual lots is called a plan.

_____10. The average number of units in a development is referred to as the development's gross density.

_____11. A restrictive covenant is considered a reasonable, legal restraint if it protects property values or restricts the free transfer of property.

_____12. The Interstate Land Sales Full Disclosure Act requires developers of any property to file a disclosure statement with HUD.

WRITE YOUR CORRECTIONS BELOW:

_____

_____

_____

_____

_____

_____

_____

_____

_____

_____

_____

_____

Multiple Choice

1. A restrictive covenant is included in the deeds for all properties in the Liberty Cove subdivision, which was built in 1962. The covenant bans "all outdoor structures designed for the storage of equipment or as habitations for any animals for 32 years from the date recorded on the original plat of subdivision." In 1997, a resident built a toolshed and a doghouse. Do the neighbors have any recourse?

    a. Yes; they can go to court and sue for monetary damages for violating the covenant.
    b. Yes; they can go to court and be awarded injunctive relief.
    c. No; the restrictive covenant is no longer operative unless the property owners of Liberty Cove have agreed to its extension.
    d. No; restrictive covenants such as this are usually considered to be unenforceable restrictions on the free transfer of property.

2. A state delegates zoning powers to a municipality through:

    a. its police power.
    b. eminent domain.
    c. a comprehensive plan.
    d. an enabling act.

3. All of the following would be included in a zoning ordinance, *EXCEPT:*

    a. permissible height and style of new construction.
    b. objectives for future development of the area.
    c. style and appearance of structures.
    d. the maximum allowable ratio of land area to structural area.

4. Which of the following protects a property owner against being deprived of his or her property by the government without just compensation?

   a. The Preamble to the U.S. Constitution
   b. The "takings clause" of the Fifth Amendment to the U.S. Constitution
   c. The "due process" clause of the Fourteenth Amendment to the U.S. Constitution
   d. The "compensation clause" of Article VII of the Bill of Rights

5. The city of Onion Lake has passed a new zoning ordinance that prohibits all commercial structures over 30 feet high. *R* wants to build an office building that will be 45 feet high. Under these facts, which of the following statements is true?

   a. *R* must apply for a nonconforming use permit.
   b. *R* must apply for a zoning permit.
   c. *R* must apply for a conditional-use permit.
   d. *R* must apply for a variance.

6. *L* would like to operate a plant-sitting business in his home, but he lives in an area zoned for residential use only. What should *L* do?

   a. Request that the zoning board declare his home to be a nonconforming use
   b. Ask a court to grant an injunction against the zoning board
   c. Seek a conditional-use permit from the zoning board
   d. Apply to the zoning board for a variance

7. *N* goes all over the country buying large tracts of vacant land, splitting them into smaller parcels and building identical communities of single-family ranch-style homes surrounding a central shopping center. *N* sells the homes to residents and leases space in the shopping center to merchants. *N* is a:

   a. developer.
   b. subdivider.
   c. developer and subdivider.
   d. developer or subdivider, but not both.

8. Which of the following best defines density zoning?

   a. The mandatory use of clustering
   b. The average number of units in a development
   c. A restriction on the average number of houses per acre
   d. A restriction on the average number of acres per parcel

9. Large lots, wide streets and uniformity are characteristic of:

   a. clustering.
   b. the curvilinear system.
   c. the gridiron pattern.
   d. aesthetic zoning ordinances.

10. All of the following are common characteristics of a constitutionally valid zoning ordinance, *EXCEPT:*

    a. clear and specific provisions.
    b. anticipation of future housing needs.
    c. nondiscriminatory effect.
    d. equal application.

11. *P* owns Heron's Nest, a 2,000-acre tract of undeveloped woodland surrounding a scenic lake in the state of North Virginia. *P* has divided the tract into 106 individual lots, ranging in size from 15 to 100 acres. P has hired several telemarketers to sell the lots to residents of North Virginia and the three states with which it shares a common border. Based on these facts, which of the following statements is true?

    a. *P* must file a disclosure statement with HUD under the Interstate Land Sales Full Disclosure Act.
    b. Because *P*'s project is not fraudulent, it is exempt from the requirements of the Interstate Land Sales Full Disclosure Act.
    c. The Heron's Nest project is exempt from the Interstate Land Sales Full Disclosure Act because of the lot size exemption, but it must comply with any state subdivided land sales laws.
    d. *P*'s project is exempt from the Interstate Land Sales Full Disclosure Act because it is not being marketed outside a contiguous multistate region, although it must comply with the subdivided land sales laws of each of the states in which it is actively marketed.

Illustration

The city of New Finedime is divided into three sections for zoning purposes: a commercial use zone, a residential use zone and an industrial use zone. In Figure 19.1, label the three zones on the map, and use the coordinates (the upper right corner is M-12) to answer the questions.

Figure 19.1   Zoning in New Finedime

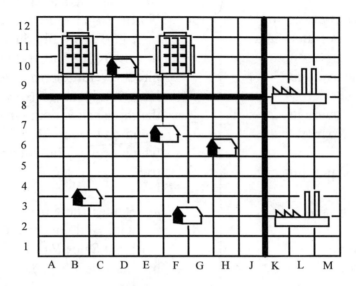

1. *M* owns a piece of property that includes areas J-8, J-9 and K-8. How can *M* use this property?

2. What would be necessary for a day-care center to obtain to operate legally at D-5?

3. Where would it be most beneficial for New Finedime to place a park as a buffer zone?

4. If New Finedime re-zones the area bounded by K-9, K-12, M-12 and M-9 as commercial, what issue might arise for a factory owner in the affected area?

5. The house at D-10 was built prior to New Finedime's zoning ordinance. How would you describe it? Through what process is it permitted to continue being a residence?

6. New Finedime's planners have asked you where they should locate a new "retail and professional services zone," which will take up 6 square units on the map. Where would you locate this new zone? Why?

KEY
220

20 Fair Housing and Ethical Practices

Chapter Summary

1. The _____ prohibits discrimination on the basis of race, color, religion, sex, handicap, familial status or national origin in real estate transactions.

2. Failure to comply with fair housing laws can result in fines and subject a licensee to _____ .

3. _____ refers to the presence of one or more individuals who have not reached the age of 18 and who live with either a parent or guardian.

4. A _____ is a physical or mental impairment.

5. The Americans with Disabilities Act requires _____ in employment and access to goods, services and public buildings.

6. _____ discrimination involves purposefully engaging in blockbusting, steering or other unfair activities.

7. Regulations established by the Department of _____ prohibit indicating a preference or limitation in advertisements for the sale or rental of property.

8. Refusing to make mortgage loans or issue insurance policies in specific areas for reasons other than an applicant's financial qualifications is _____ .

9. _____ refers to a system of moral principles, rules and standards of conduct.

10. A written standard for professional conduct is known as a _____.

Key Term Matching

1. A law that prohibits discrimination in housing based on race, color, religion and national origin

2. The Civil Rights Act of 1968, the Housing and Community Development Act of 1974 and the Fair Housing Amendments Act of 1988, collectively

3. The agency that administers the federal fair housing laws

4. The presence of one or more persons who are under the age of 18, living with a parent or adult guardian

5. A physical or mental impairment

6. A U.S. Supreme Court decision that established the doctrine of "separate but equal" regarding race

7. A U.S. Supreme Court decision that prohibits all racial discrimination in housing

8. A law that prohibits discrimination against protected classes in evaluating loan applicants

9. A law that requires accessibility to employment, goods and services for individuals with disabilities

10. Encouraging the sale or renting of property by claiming a protected class of people are moving into the area

11. Encouraging home seekers to limit their search to particular neighborhoods based on noneconomic factors

_____ ADA

_____ blockbusting

_____ Civil Rights Act of 1968

_____ disability

_____ Equal Credit Opportunity Act

_____ Fair Housing Act

_____ familial status

_____ HUD

_____ *Jones v. Mayer*

_____ *Plessy v. Ferguson*

_____ steering

True and False

_____ 1. The purpose of the civil rights laws that affect the real estate industry is to make everyone equal.

_____ 2. Failing to comply with state and federal fair housing laws may subject a licensee to both fines and disciplinary action.

_____ 3. The Civil Rights Act of 1866 applies only to race.

_____ 4. The Civil Rights Act of 1968 applies only to race.

_____ 5. Under HUD regulations, a "dwelling" is limited to single family houses, condominiums and cooperatives.

_____ 6. Persons with AIDS are protected by the fair housing laws under the "disabled persons" classification.

_____ 7. There are no exemptions under the federal Fair Housing Act.

_____ 8. The protections under the Equal Credit Opportunity Act are broader than those under the Fair Housing Act.

_____ 9. The ADA's specific requirements for making curb ramps, elevators and other spaces accessible for people with disabilities are contained in the "Accessibility Guidelines."

_____ 10. Redlining is the act of encouraging people to sell or rent their homes on the basis that the entry of members of a protected class into the neighborhood will reduce property values.

_____ 11. Channeling home seekers to particular neighborhoods based on noneconomic factors is a practice known as steering.

_____ 12. There are no exceptions to HUD's rules regarding statements of preference or limitations in advertising regarding race.

_____ 13. While not valid considerations for the underlying real estate transaction, the following factors may be considered by an appraiser in evaluating a property: race, color, religion, national origin, sex, disability and familial status.

_____ 14. Any individual who believes he or she is the victim of illegal discrimination in a real estate transaction may file a complaint with HUD within three years of the alleged act.

_____ 15. Once a complaint of discrimination in housing has been received by HUD, it must be resolved in a formal administrative proceeding before an administrative law judge.

_____ 16. Complaints brought under the Civil Rights Act of 1866 are taken directly to the Office of Fair Housing and Equal Opportunity for investigation and resolution.

_____ 17. The Fair Housing Amendments Act of 1988 established a "Code of Ethics" for real estate licensees and other participants in real estate transactions.

WRITE YOUR CORRECTIONS BELOW:

_____

_____

_____

_____

_____

_____

_____

_____

_____

Multiple Choice

1. Which of the following offer protection against discrimination in housing on the basis of race, color, religion and national origin only?

   a. Fair Housing Act
   b. Fair Housing Amendments Act of 1988
   c. Housing and Community Development Act of 1974
   d. Civil Rights Act of 1968

2. The Fair Housing Act is administered by:

   a. ADAAG.
   b. HUD.
   c. OFHEO.
   d. the federal court system.

3. The Fair Housing Act prohibits discrimination on the basis of all the following factors, *EXCEPT:*

   a. familial status.
   b. national origin.
   c. religious preference.
   d. sexual preference.

4. To raise a little grocery money, *R* decides to rent a spare bedroom in her single-family house to a tenant for $50 per month. When a 24-year-old man asks to see the room, *R* refuses, telling him that she will only rent to women over the age of 50. The prospective tenant threatens to sue for a violation of the Fair Housing Act. Should *R* be concerned?

   a. Yes; the amount of rent being charged is immaterial for purposes of the Fair Housing Act.
   b. Yes; while *R* is permitted to exclude individuals on the basis of age or sex, she cannot exclude on the basis of both.
   c. No; the rental of rooms in an owner-occupied single-family home is exempt from the Fair Housing Act.
   d. No; because there was no real estate licensee involved in this transaction, *R* is free to discriminate on the basis of any of the normally protected classes.

5. The Equal Credit Opportunity Act prohibits discrimination on the basis of all of the following factors, *EXCEPT:*

   a. amount of income.
   b. source of income.
   c. marital status.
   d. age.

6. While real estate licensees may be ethically obligated to be aware of the requirements of the ADA, they may also have a legal obligation to comply with the act, because licensees:

   a. often have clients with disabilities.
   b. frequently own their own homes.
   c. may be employers.
   d. are required to do so by the Code of Ethics.

7. *W*, a real estate broker, sends a bright yellow flier to all the homeowners in the Grayside Hills neighborhood. The flier contains a reprinted article from a local newspaper describing the future relocation plans of various employers in the region and the following statement, printed in bold red letters: "WARNING! THE FAILURE TO SELL YOUR PROPERTY WITHIN THE NEXT SIX MONTHS COULD COST YOU A BUNDLE!" At the bottom of the page was printed *W*'s name, photo, office address and phone number. Based on these fact, which of the following statements is true?

   a. W is guilty of steering.
   b. W is guilty of blockbusting.
   c. W has committed no offense.
   d. W has violated the HUD advertising guidelines.

8. In the past six months, a local bank has been forced to foreclose on several mortgages in the mostly Asian suburb of Grand Pasture. The bank's board of directors tells the loan department to make no further loans on properties located in the suburb. Based on these facts, which of the following statements is true?

   a. The bank is guilty of redlining.
   b. The bank is in violation of the Home Mortgage Disclosure Act.
   c. The bank's action falls under the "reasonable purpose" exception to the Fair Housing Act.
   d. The bank is guilty of discrimination on the basis of race.

9. *M* and *N* are real estate brokers. *M* places a newspaper ad for a property that says, "Features a lovely bay window perfect for a piano or the Christmas tree." *N*'s ad on the Internet says, "Male roommate sought for w-alk-up apartment in good neighborhood." Which of these brokers have violated HUD's advertising guidelines?

   a. *M* and *N* have both violated the guidelines.
   b. *M* only; *M*'s ad violates the rule against stating a religious preference.
   c. *N* only; *N*'s ad violates the rule against stating an explicit preference based on sex
   d. Neither *M* nor *N* has violated the guidelines.

10. Because the region in which broker *C* works has homeowners of many different ethnic backgrounds, *C* took a three-week intensive course called "Understanding a Diverse Market." In the course, *C* learned about the cultural habits of people from a wide variety of countries and cultures. Now, when a prospective buyer from far-off Thabong or the highlands of Nyenska comes into *C*'s office, *C* knows just which neighborhood they'd feel most comfortable living in and helps them adjust to life in the U.S. by showing them properties exclusively in areas where there are other homeowners from their homelands. Based on these facts only, *C*:

   a. is in violation of the Civil Rights Act of 1964.
   b. is committing steering, but is not guilty due to the lack of discriminatory effect.
   c. is guilty of steering.
   d. is not guilty of steering, because C lacks a discriminatory intent.

11. What is the statute of limitations for housing discrimination actions brought under the Civil Rights Act of 1866?

   a. 100 days
   b. 1 year
   c. 2 years
   d. The same as the statute of limitations for torts committed in the state in which the alleged discriminatory act occurred

12. Complaints of discriminatory housing practices filed with HUD will be referred to a local enforcement agency if:

    a. the federal law is substantially more inclusive than the state or municipal law.
    b. HUD determines that an administrative law judge should decide the case.
    c. the state or municipal law is substantially equivalent to the federal law.
    d. the complaint involves a licensee who is the victim of a threat or act of violence because he or she has complied with the fair housing laws.

13. The term "professional ethics" refers to:

    a. the system of professional standards adopted by the National Association of REALTORS® in 1913.
    b. the requirements of the Fair Housing Act as they apply to real estate professionals.
    c. a system of moral principles, rules and standards of conduct that govern a professional's relations with consumers and colleagues.
    d. a standard of integrity and competence expected of professionals and licensees in the housing and real estate industry, established by the Department of Housing and Urban Development, symbolized by the equal housing opportunity poster.

Illustration

In Figure 20.1, complete the diagram by filling in the name of the correct federal law in each square, based on the protections against discrimination it creates. In the appropriate circles, write the names of the two important U.S. Supreme Court cases discussed in Chapter 20.

Figure 20.1   ## The Evolution of Fair Housing Law

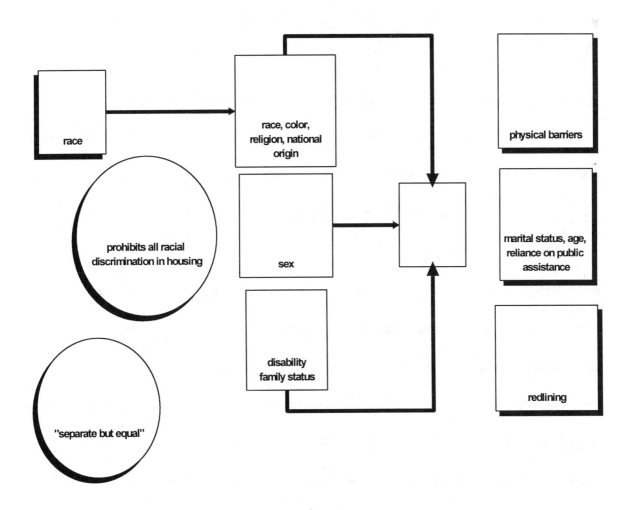

21 Environmental Issues and the Real Estate Transaction

Chapter Summary

1. Prior to 1978, _____ insulation was used in most residences.

2. Elevated levels of _____ in the human body can cause serious damage to the brain, kidneys, nervous system and red blood cells.

3. The EPA and HUD require that known _____ hazards be disclosed to purchasers of residential housing constructed prior to 1978.

4. _____ is a naturally occurring gas that is suspected of causing lung cancer.

5. While there is scientific evidence that _____ insulation causes cancer in animals, proof of its effect on humans has been found insufficient to support a ban.

6. Furnaces, water heaters and wood stoves all produce _____ as a natural result of burning fuel.

7. The _____ fields produced by high-voltage power lines are suspected by some of causing a variety of health problems.

8. Federal, state and local regulations govern the construction, content and, content and maintenance of _____ sites.

9. "Superfund" is a federal program established by the _____

   Act in 1980 and 1986 to clean up uncontrolled hazardous-waste sites and spills.

10. While _____ are not expected to be environmental experts,

    they may still be liable for failing to disclose known environmental hazards.

Key Term Matching

1. A highly friable mineral commonly used as insulation prior to being banned in 1978

2. The process of sealing off a hazardous material without removing it

3. A material once used in paint that can cause serious brain and nervous system damage

4. A radioactive gas produced by the natural decay of other underground radioactive substances

5. An insulating foam material that can release harmful gases

6. A by-product of electrical currents that may pose a health risk

7. The natural level at which the ground is saturated

8. A site for the burial of waste.

9. The party held liable for clean-up costs by EPA under CERCLA

10. The process of covering a solid waste site with topsoil and plants

11. Money set aside by the Comprehensive Environmental Response, Compensation and Liability Act to pay for the clean up of uncontrolled hazardous waste sites

_____ asbestos

_____ capping

_____ electromagnetic field

_____ encapsulation

_____ landfill

_____ lead

_____ PRP

_____ radon

_____ Superfund

_____ urea-formaldehyde

_____ water table

True and False

_____ 1. The Environmental Protection Agency estimates that approximately 20 percent of commercial and public buildings built after 1978 contain asbestos insulation.

_____ 2. Asbestos removal is a relatively simple, inexpensive process that can be performed by any reasonably intelligent person.

_____ 3. Under the 1996 regulations published by the Environmental Protection Agency and the Department of Housing and Urban Development, owners of homes built prior to 1978 are required to test their properties for the presence of lead-based paint and must fill out a lead-based paint disclosure statement.

_____ 4. Radon is a naturally-occurring substance that is suspected of being a cause of lung cancer.

_____ 5. Urea-formaldehyde foam insulation has not been proven harmful to humans.

_____ 6. Electromagnetic fields are created by the movement of electricity through high-tension power lines, secondary distribution lines, electrical transformers and clock radios.

_____ 7. Groundwater is water that lies on the earth's surface.

_____ 8. Underground storage tanks involved in the collection of storm water or wastewater are exempt from federal regulations.

_____ 9. The process of laying two to four feet of soil over the top of a landfill site and then planting foliage to prevent erosion is referred to as "layering."

_____10. Liability under Superfund is strict, joint and several, and retroactive.

WRITE YOUR CORRECTIONS BELOW:

_____

_____

_____

_____

_____

_____

_____

_____

_____

_____

Multiple Choice

1. Prior to 1978, asbestos was a component of more than 3,000 types of building materials, and is currently present in what percentage of commercial and public buildings in the United States?

   a. 10 percent
   b. 12 percent
   c. 20 percent
   d. 33 percent

2. Lead is commonly found in all of the following, *EXCEPT:*

   a. water pipes.
   b. alkyd oil-based paint.
   c. automobile exhaust.
   d. insulating material.

3. *J* accepts an offer from *K* on her vintage Victorian home, built in 1892. Based on these facts, all of the following statements are true, *EXCEPT*:

   a. *J* must attach a lead-based paint disclosure statement to the sales contract.
   b. If *J* is aware of any lead-based paint on the premises, she must disclose that fact to *K*.
   c. If *K* requests a lead-based paint inspection, *J* has 10 days in which to obtain one at her own expense.
   d. *K* is entitled to receive a pamphlet that describes the hazards posed by lead-based paint.

4. Where in the United States does radon occur?

   a. Mostly in the western states
   b. Mostly in the warm southern and southwestern regions
   c. Throughout the United States
   d. Only in large urban areas

5. All of the following have been proven to pose a health hazard, *EXCEPT*:

   a. asbestos.
   b. electromagnetic fields.
   c. lead-based paint.
   d. radon.

6. *H* stores toxic chemical waste in a large steel tank that has only fifteen percent of its volume underground. *J* lives far out in the wilderness and has her own gas pump connected to a 1,000-gallon tank of gasoline buried ten feet underground near her garage. *L* keeps three large tanks filled with formaldehyde and battery acid in his basement. Which of these people are *NOT* exempt from federal regulations regarding USTs?

   a. *H, J* and *L*   c. *L* only
   b. *J* and *L* only   d. *H* only

7. Which of the following is responsible for administering Superfund?

   a. CERCLA   c. EPA
   b. PRP   d. HUD

8. Proof of all of the following is necessary for innocent landowner immunity, *EXCEPT*:

   a. the pollution was caused by a third party.
   b. the landowner exercised "due care" when the property was purchased.
   c. the landowner is a lender who acquired the property as a result of foreclosure.
   d. the landowner had no actual or constructive knowledge of the damage.

9. In 1972, the *PKL* Chemical Company owned Graylake and used both the lake and surrounding woodland as a dumping ground for millions of gallons of toxic waste chemicals. In 1979, *PKL* sold the property to *D*, its vice-president, who built the Graylake Office Park. In 1990, *D* sold the development to *H*, who tore down the offices and built the Waterland Fun Park. *H* borrowed half of the $500,000 purchase price from Big Bank. In 1996, the EPA informed *H* that the Fun Park was built on a toxic dump and that the lake was a bubbling stew of deadly chemicals. Clean-up costs would be nearly $1 billion. Based on these facts, who is responsible for clean-up under SARA?

   a. *PKL*, *D* and *H* only; lenders are immune under SARA.
   b. H only; retroactivity does not apply under these facts.
   c. *PKL*, *D*, *H* and Big Bank are jointly, severally and retroactively liable, although *H* and Big Bank may have innocent landowner immunity.
   d. *PKL*, *D*, *H* and Big Bank are jointly, severally and retroactively liable, and the strict liability imposed by CERCLA prohibits any immunities under SARA.

10. If a PRP refuses to pay the expenses of cleaning up a toxic site, the EPA:

    a. may bring a criminal action and have the PRP jailed for up to ten years.
    b. may bring a civil action and be awarded three times the actual cost of the clean-up.
    c. may bring an administrative action and be awarded the actual cost of the clean-up, plus court costs.
    d. has no legal recourse.

Illustration

Figure 21.1, identify where each of the environmental hazards or issues listed would occur by writing the number of the item in the appropriate circle.

Figure 21.1   **Environmental Concerns in Residential Real Estate**

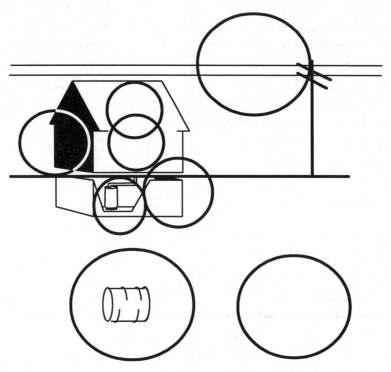

1. Asbestos
2. Carbon monoxide
3. EMF
4. Groundwater contamination
5. Lead paint
6. UFFI
7. LUSTs

KEY
225

22 Closing the Real Estate Transaction

Chapter Summary

1. _____ is the point at which ownership of property is transferred in exchange for the selling price.

2. Shortly before the closing takes place, the buyer usually will make a final inspection of the property, accompanied by the agent, called a "_____".

3. A _____ gives the purchaser information about the exact location and size of the property.

4. In an _____ closing, a third party coordinates closing activities on behalf of both the buyer and the seller.

5. Every real estate transaction must be reported to the Internal Revenue Service by the closing agent on a form _____.

6. _____ is a federal law designed to protect consumers from abusive lending practices and to ensure that consumers receive complete, accurate information about the actual costs of the transaction.

7. The _____ or HUD-1 form itemizes all charges to be paid by the buyer and seller in connection with a real estate settlement.

8. In a closing statement, a _____ is an amount to be paid by the buyer or seller; a _____ is an amount that is payable to the buyer or seller.

9. _____ items, such as interest on an assumed mortgage, are a

   buyer credit owed by the seller that will be paid later by the buyer.

10. Interest on most mortgage loans is paid in _____, so a payment

    due for any particular month includes the interest due for the previous month.

Key Term Matching

1. The consummation of a real estate transaction

2. A method of closing in which a disinterested third party acts as the agent of both buyer and seller to coordinate the closing activities

3. The type of loan governed by RESPA

4. A charge that a party owes and must pay at closing

5. An amount that has already been paid, that is being reimbursed or that will be paid in the future

6. The division of financial responsibility for various items between the buyer and seller

7. Charges owed by the seller that will be paid by the buyer

8. Charges that have been paid by and are credited to the seller

9. A 360-day period used in calculating prorations

10. An unearned fee, paid as part of a real estate transaction, that is prohibited by RESPA

_____ accrued items

_____ banking year

_____ closing

_____ credit

_____ debit

_____ escrow

_____ federally-related

_____ kickback

_____ prepaid items

_____ proration

True and False

_____ 1.   At closing, the terms of the sales contract are fulfilled and the mortgage loan funds (if any) are distributed to the buyer.

_____ 2.   Shortly before the closing takes place, the buyer will usually conduct a final inspection of the property, usually called a "spot survey."

_____ 3.   While the particulars of closing in escrow vary from state to state, the escrow agent is always a licensed attorney.

_____ 4.   When closing in escrow, the seller will deposit proof of hazard insurance with the escrow agent.

_____ 5.   All real estate transactions must be reported to the IRS by the seller's broker on a form 1099-S.

_____ 6.   RESPA applies to all federally-related loans, except for those administered by HUD.

_____ 7.   Real estate licensees are exempt from RESPA's rules governing controlled business arrangements and referrals.

_____ 8.   A special HUD information booklet must be provided to all real estate loan applicants.

_____ 9.   Borrowers have the right to inspect the completed HUD-1 form ten days prior to closing.

_____ 10. RESPA's rules prohibit both paying and receiving a kickback.

WRITE YOUR CORRECTIONS BELOW:

_____

_____

_____

Multiple Choice

For Questions 1 through 4, prorate using a 30-day month and a 360-day year; prorate the taxes as of the close of escrow. Split the escrow fee 50-50 between the parties. Use the following relevant facts:

- Purchase price: $25,000 cash
- Earnest money: $1,000
- Commission rate: 7 percent
- Revenue stamps: $25
- Real estate taxes: $350 paid in full for the current year
- Title insurance policy: $153.51
- Recording fee: $2
- Escrow fee: $168
- Existing mortgage loan balance: $9,450, including credit for the reserve account
- Closing date: July 31

1. What amount is the buyer debited for the real estate taxes?

   a. $145.83   c. $202.19
   b. $146.71   d. $203.30

2. What amount is the seller debited for the broker's commission?

   a. $750   c. $1,750
   b. $1,650   d. $2,500

3. What amount of the escrow fee will the buyer pay?

   a. $56   c. $160
   b. $84   d. $168

4. What is the real estate commission in this transaction?

   a. $1,750   c. $1,780
   b. $1,754   d. $1,790

5. A sale is closing on August 31. Real estate taxes, calculated on a calendar year basis, have not been paid for the current year. The tax is estimated to be $1,800. What amount of proration will be credited to the buyer?

   a. $1,100   c. $1,485
   b. $1,200   d. $1,500

6. A seller would be responsible for providing all of the following items, *EXCEPT*:

   a. evidence of title.
   b. affidavits of title.
   c. the deed.
   d. documentation for a new loan.

7. *Q* is purchasing 345 Minor Street from *G*. The single-family home is subject to an existing 30-year mortgage of $86,500 at a fixed rate of 6 percent. Under the terms of the sales contract, *Q* will assume *G*'s mortgage at 6 percent interest, and pay the federally-insured lender's standard assumption fee of $75. In addition, *G* will assist *Q* by taking back a purchase-money mortgage in

the amount of $25,000 at 8 percent interest. Is this transaction subject to RESPA?

a. No, because this transaction involves a purchase-money mortgage taken back by the seller.
b. No, because the terms of the assumed loan are modified and the lender's fee exceeds $50.
c. Yes, because the seller is taking back a purchase-money mortgage at an interest rate higher than that charged for the assumed loan.
d. Yes, because the terms of the assumed loan are modified and the lender's fee exceeds $50.

8. Since 1972, *M*, a real estate broker, has had an understanding with two of the five mortgage lenders in town. *M* recommends only those two lenders to her clients and does not tell clients about any other lenders. In return, the recommended lenders pay for the vacations *M* offers her salespeople as rewards for high performance. Based on these facts, which of the following statements is true?

a. *M* is not doing anything illegal.
b. Because this arrangement has been in existence for more than fifteen years, it is exempt from RESPA.
c. This is a permissible controlled business arrangement under RESPA, because *M* is not paid a fee for the recommendations.
d. *M*'s arrangement with the lenders is an illegal kickback under RESPA.

9. How long must a lender retain a HUD-1 after the date of closing?

a. six months   c. two years
b. one year   d. four years

10. *L* owns a fully-occupied rental apartment building. If *L* sells the apartment building to *K*, how will the tenant's security deposits be reflected on the closing statement?

a. Credit *L*, debit *K*
b. Debit both *L* and *K*
c. Credit *K*, debit *L*
d. Security deposits are not reflected on a closing statement.

11. All of the following items are usually prorated at closing, *EXCEPT*:

a. prepaid general real estate taxes.
b. interest on an assumed loan.
c. appraisal fees.
d. rents.

For questions 12 through 14, prorate using the actual number of days in the month and year. Split the escrow fee 50-50. The purchaser assumes the existing mortgage balance of $127,042.42; the purchaser will pay cash at the closing in the amount of the difference between the purchase price and the loan balance; the present monthly payment on the loan is $1,101.40. Closing is October 15. Other facts:

- Purchase price: $350,000
- Earnest money: $3,500
- Commission rate: 6 percent split 50-50
- Real estate taxes: $2,900 paid in full for the current year
- Escrow fee: $800
- Title insurance policy: $1,150
- Insurance policy: $758 annual premium
- Revenue stamps: $126.30
- Recording fee: $30
- Interest rate: 8.75 percent, with the next payment due on November 1

12. What are the prorated real estate taxes to be charged to the buyer?

    a. $608.06   c. $690.67
    b. $611.77   d. $728.30

13. What will be the amount of commission paid to the cooperating broker?

    a. $8,750   c. $17,500
    b. $10,500   d. $21,000

14. What amount will the seller receive at the closing?

    a. $200,581.15   c. $208,654.34
    b. $205,572.33   d. $217,749.28

Illustration

In Figure 22.1, complete the settlement statement worksheet based on the information provided below. Carry out all computations to three decimal places until the final calculation. Prorate based on a 30-day month. The buyer's and seller's statements should be viewed separately, although many items will appear on both. Although both the buyer's and the seller's total debits and credits must balance, their totals and cash due need not. Selling price for the property is $115,000; the earnest money deposit is $12,000.

Buyers: Doug and Gonnie Cornwall
Seller: Cordelia Lear
Property address: 1604 North Albany
Closing date: June 30 of the current year
Broker's commission: 7 percent
Property taxes: $1,750/year; this year's taxes have not yet been paid
Payoff existing loan: $43,000 balance of principal and accrued interest
Financing: buyer is obtaining a new $82,000 first mortgage loan

Loan origination fee: $2,460 (3 points); paid by buyer
Transfer tax: $.50 per $500; paid by seller
Recording fees: $10.00 per document (deed and new mortgage paid by buyer; release of mortgage paid by seller)
Attorney's fees: $300 buyer; $450 seller
Title insurance: owner's policy, cost: $700 (seller); mortgagee's policy $150 (buyer)
Document preparation: $50; paid by buyer
Survey: $150; paid by seller

Figure 22.1   Closing Statement

PROPERTY:_____

SELLER:_____

BUYER:_____

SETTLEMENT DATE:_____

	BUYER'S STATEMENT		SELLER'S STATEMENT	
	DEBIT	CREDIT	DEBIT	CREDIT
TOTALS				
DUE FROM BUYER				
DUE TO SELLER				

Answer Key

Chapter 1

CHAPTER SUMMARY

1. brokerage
2. REALTORS®
3. residential, commercial, industrial, agricultural or special-purpose
4. market
5. supply and demand

KEY TERM MATCHING

4   broker
5   brokerage
6   demand
1   market
3   salesperson
2   supply

TRUE AND FALSE

1. *False*   The five classes of real estate mentioned in the text are residential, commercial, *industrial*, agricultural and special-purpose.
2. *True*
3. *False*   The supply of labor and the cost of construction generally have a direct effect on the *supply* of real estate in a market.
4. *True*
5. *False*   Warehouses, factories and power plants are examples of *industrial* property.
6. *False*   Members of the National Association of Real Estate Brokers are known as *Realtists*. **OR** Members of the National Association of *REALTORS*® are known as REALTORS®.

MULTIPLE CHOICE

1. a   3. a   5. b
2. b   4. d

FIGURE 1.1

Suggested solutions:

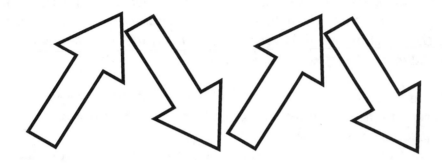

(A)	Supply	Price	Price	Demand
(B)	Demand	Supply	Supply	Price

Chapter 2

CHAPTER SUMMARY

1. Land
2. real estate
3. Real property
4. personal property
5. fixtures
6. trade
7. economic
8. physical
9. bundle
10. licensing

KEY TERM MATCHING

3 accession
6 air rights
4 bundle of legal rights
9 fixture
10 improvement
2 personal property

7 real estate
5 real property
11 severance
8 subsurface rights
12 surface rights
1 trade fixture

TRUE AND FALSE

1. *False* The terms "land," "real estate" and "real property" are not interchangeable: they refer to *different aspects* of the same thing.
2. *False* "*Land*" is defined as the earth's surface extending downward to the center of the earth and upward to infinity, including permanent natural objects such as trees and water. *OR* "Real property" is *defined as the interests, benefits and rights inherent in the ownership of real estate.*
3. *True*
4. *False* The transfer of the right to use the surface of the earth does not necessarily include the right to the natural resources that lie beneath the surface of the earth, known as *subsurface rights*.
5. *False* Trees, perennial shrubbery and grasses that do not require annual cultivation are considered *real* property.
6. *True*
7. *True*
8. *False* The *economic* characteristics of land are scarcity, improvements, permanence of investment and area preference.
9. *False* Immobility, indestructibility and *uniqueness* are physical characteristics of *land*.
10. *True*

MULTIPLE CHOICE

1. b
2. d
3. b
4. d

5. b
6. d
7. b
8. b

ILLUSTRATIONS

FIGURE 2.1

Control
Disposition
Enjoyment
Exclusion
Possession

FIGURE 2.2

		Real Property	Personal Property	Fixture	Trade Fixture
1	Sidewalks and sewers in a subdivision	✔			
2	Bushes surrounding a residence	✔			
3	Wheat or corn crops on a farm		✔		
4	Kitchen sink installed in a home	✔		✔	
5	Booths in a restaurant installed by a tenant		✔		✔
6	Curtains installed by a tenant		✔		
7	Pumps installed by a gas station tenant		✔		✔
8	Machinery installed by landowner	✔		✔	

Chapter 3 ▮▮▮

CHAPTER SUMMARY

1. proprietary lease
2. deduct
3. deferred
4. 55; $125,000
5. insurance
6. Converted-use properties
7. Modular
8. principal, interest, tax and insurance
9. coinsurance; 80
10. federal or federally related

KEY TERM MATCHING

9	adjusted basis	2	cooperative
1	apartment complex	7	equity
4	capital gain	10	mixed-use development (MUD)
5	condominium	6	planned unit development (PUD)
8	coinsurance	3	standard homeowner's insurance

TRUE AND FALSE

1. *False* A *condominium* is a form of residential ownership in which residents share ownership of common areas while owning their own units individually.

2. *False* Warehouses, factories, office buildings, hotels and other structures that have been remodeled to residential use are referred to as *converted-use properties*.

3. *True*

4. *True*

5. *True*

6. *True*

7. *False* Taxpayers over the age of 55 are entitled to a one-time *exclusion* from taxation of up to $125,000 of the gain from the sale or exchange of their principal residence.

8. *True*

9. *False* Under standard homeowner's insurance policies, the insured is usually required to maintain insurance equal to at least *80 percent* of the replacement cost of the dwelling, excluding the price of the land.

10. *False* If a borrower's property is located in a designated flood area, *it may be exempt from the National Flood Insurance Act's flood insurance requirement if the borrower can produce a survey showing that the lowest part of the structure is above the 100-year flood mark.*

MULTIPLE CHOICE

1.	c	7.	c
2.	d	8.	a
3.	a	9.	c
4.	c	10.	c
5.	a	11.	a
6.	d		

ILLUSTRATION

Figure 3.1

Cooperative	PUD
Converted Use	MUD *or* Condominium
Condominium	Rental Apartment Complex

Chapter 4 |||

CHAPTER SUMMARY

1. agency
2. implied
3. single
4. subagents
5. common
6. nonagent OR transactional agent
7. dual agency
8. does not
9. customers
10. honest

KEY TERM MATCHING, Part I

6   agency
3   agent
9   customer
8   general agent
4   implied agreement
1   law of agency
10 non-agent
5   principal
7   puffing
2   special agent

KEY TERM MATCHING, Part II

3   buyer's brokers
6   client
8   common law duties
7   disclosed dual agency
2   express agreement
10 latent defect
5   stigmatized property
9   subagent
1   undisclosed dual agency
4   universal agent

TRUE AND FALSE

1. *False*   The individual who hires and delegates to the agent the responsibility of representing his or her other interests is the *principal*.
2. *True*
3. *False*   An agent works *for* the client and with the *customer*.

4. *True*

5. *False*   The common-law fiduciary duty of obedience obligates the agent to act in good faith at all times and obey all the principal's *lawful and ethical* instructions.

6. *False*   The common-law duty of loyalty requires that an agent not disclose the principal's financial situation *but facts about the condition of the property must be disclosed.*

7. *False*   *Dual* agency relationships are generally illegal unless the agent receives the informed, written consent of all parties.

8. *False*   The source of compensation is *not* the key determining factor in whether or not an agency relationship exists.

9. *False*   A *universal* agent is empowered to do anything the principal could do personally, with virtually no limitation on his or her authority to act.

10. *False*   A real estate broker is usually the *special* agent of a buyer or seller.

11. *False*   *A buyer's agent owes his or her principal the same fiduciary duties as a seller's agent owes a seller.*

12. *True*

13. *False*   A dual agency relationship is legal if *both* the buyer and the seller consent to the dual representation.

14. *False*   An agent owes a *customer* the duties of reasonable care and skill, honest and fair dealing, and disclosure of known facts.

15. *False*   *Puffing* occurs when the broker engages in exaggeration of a property's benefits or features **OR** A negligent misrepresentation occurs when the broker *should have known that a statement about a material fact was false.*

16. *False*   When a property has a hidden structural defect that could not be discovered by ordinary inspection, it is referred to as *having a latent defect*.

MULTIPLE CHOICE

1.	c		6.	d	
2.	d		7.	c	
3.	a		8.	c	
4.	c		9.	c	
5.	a		10.	c	

ILLUSTRATIONS

Figure 4.1

Figure 4.2

Figure 4.3

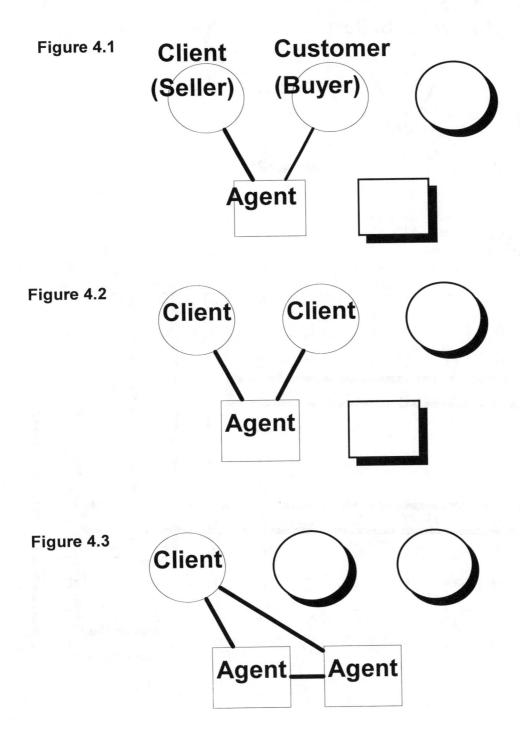

Figure 4.4

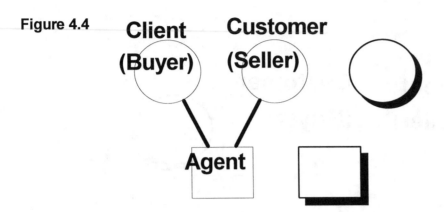

Figure 4.5

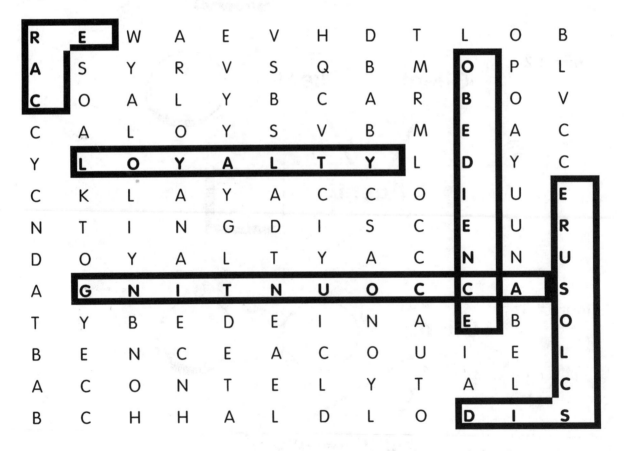

Chapter 5

CHAPTER SUMMARY

1. Real estate license laws and regulations
2. protect the public
3. Real estate brokerage
4. commission
5. ready, willing and able
6. salesperson
7. antitrust

KEY TERM MATCHING

14 allocation of markets
 4 brokerage
 1 caveat emptor
10 commission
 8 employee
13 group boycotting
 9 independent contractor
11 procuring cause

12 ready, willing and able buyer
 5 real estate broker
 2 real estate license laws
 3 rules and regulations
 7 salesperson
 6 sole proprietorship

TRUE AND FALSE

1. *False*   *All fifty* states regulate the activities of real estate brokers and salespeople.
2. *False*   The purpose of the real estate license laws is to regulate the real estate industry and protect *the rights of purchasers, sellers, tenants and owners.*
3. *False*   A real estate *broker* is licensed to buy, sell, exchange or lease real property for others, and to charge a fee for those services.
4. *False*   A real estate *salesperson* is an an individual who is licensed to perform real estate activities on behalf of a licensed broker.
5. *True*
6. *True*
7. *False*   A broker is considered the procuring cause of a sale if he or she *started a chain of events that resulted in the sale.*
8. *True*
9. *False*   The practice of setting prices for products or services is referred to as *price fixing.*
10. *True*

MULTIPLE CHOICE

1. b
2. c
3. b
4. d
5. d

6. c
7. b
8. a
9. c
10. a

ILLUSTRATIONS

Figure 5.1

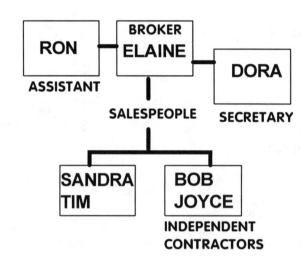

Figure 5.2 *Answers will vary, depending on state licensing laws and regulations*

▌Chapter 6

CHAPTER SUMMARY

1. employment contract
2. special
3. exclusive-right-to-sell
4. exclusive-agency
5. open
6. multiple listing service
7. net
8. option

9. termination
10. competitive market analysis
11. Market value
12. buyer agency agreement
13. exclusive
14. exclusive agency
15. open

KEY TERM MATCHING

8 CMA
11 exclusive agency buyer listing
3 exclusive-agency listing
10 exclusive buyer agency
2 exclusive-right-to-sell listing
1 listing agreement

5 MLS
6 net listing
9 open buyer agency
4 open listing
7 option listing

TRUE AND FALSE

1. *False* Under a typical net listing, the broker's commission is based on the *amount by which the sales price exceeds the seller's required net.*
2. *False* A listing agreement is *an employment contract, not* a contract for the sale of real estate.
3. *False* The parties to a listing agreement are a *broker and a seller.*
4. *False* The salesperson *helps the seller set the listing price for a property* by using a competitive market analysis.
5. *False* A listing agreement in which the seller retains the right to employ any number of brokers as agent is referred to as *an open listing.*
6. *False* In an *exclusive-agency* listing, one broker is authorized to act as the exclusive agent of the principal, who retains the right to sell the property without obligation to the broker.
7. *False* In buyer agency, the source of compensation is *not* the major factor that determines the relationship.
8. *True*
9. *False* In an exclusive buyer agency agreement, the broker is entitled to payment *regardless of whether he or she locates the property purchased.*
10. *True*
11. *False* Because a listing agreement is a personal service contract between a broker and seller, *the broker may not transfer the listing to another broker without the seller's written consent.*
12. *False* A listing agreement *should include* such details as which items of personal property stay with the real estate, or the disposition of leased equipment.

MULTIPLE CHOICE

1. d
2. a
3. a
4. d
5. d
6. c
7. c
8. b
9. c
10. d

ILLUSTRATIONS

Figure 6.1 *Open Listing*
Figure 6.2 *Exclusive Agency Listing*
Figure 6.3 *Exclusive Right to Sell Listing*

Figure 6.4 *Answers may vary, depending on measurements and descriptions of the property and its features.*

Chapter 7

CHAPTER SUMMARY

1. police power
2. eminent domain
3. escheat
4. estate
5. Freehold
6. fee simple
7. curtesy, dower and homestead
8. Encumbrances
9. easement
10. Appurtenant; dominant tenement; servient tenement
11. easement in gross
12. license
13. encroachment
14. riparian
15. littoral
16. prior appropriation

KEY TERM MATCHING, Part I

3 condemnation
2 eminent domain
5 escheat
6 estate in land
9 fee simple absolute
10 fee simple defeasible
7 freehold estates
8 leasehold estates
1 police power
4 taxation

KEY TERM MATCHING, Part II

7 deed restriction
8 easement
9 encroachment
5 encumbrance
4 homestead
6 lien
2 life estate pur autre vie
10 prior appropriation
3 remainderman
1 right of reentry

TRUE AND FALSE

1. *False*   A state's power to enact legislation that preserves order, protects the public health and safety and promotes the general welfare is referred to as its *police power*.
2. *True*
3. *False*   The process by which the government exercises its right to acquire privately owned real estate for public use through either judicial or administrative proceedings is called *condemnation*.
4. *False*   The purpose of escheat is to *prevent property from being ownerless or abandoned*.
5. *False*   A *fee simple estate* is the highest interest in real estate recognized by law.
6. *True*
7. *False*   If the grantor is silent about what happens to property after a life estate ends, the grantor has a *reversionary* interest in the property.
8. *True*
9. *False*   An appurtenant easement is said to run with the land, and transfers with the deed of the *dominant* tenement.
10. *False*   An easement that arises when an owner sells property that has no access to a street or public way except across the seller's remaining land is an easement by *necessity*.
11. *False*   The concept of "tacking" provides that successive periods of continuous occupation by different parties may be combined to reach the required total number of years necessary to establish a claim for an *easement by prescription*.
12. *True*
13. *True*
14. *False*   Riparian and littoral rights are *attached to the land: the right to use the water belongs to whomever owns the bordering land*.
15. *True*

MULTIPLE CHOICE

1. b
2. c
3. b
4. d
5. d

6. c
7. b
8. a
9. c
10. c

ILLUSTRATIONS

Figure 7.1

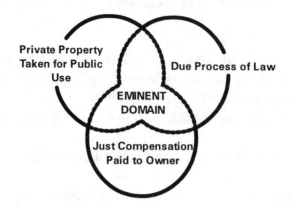

Figure 7.2

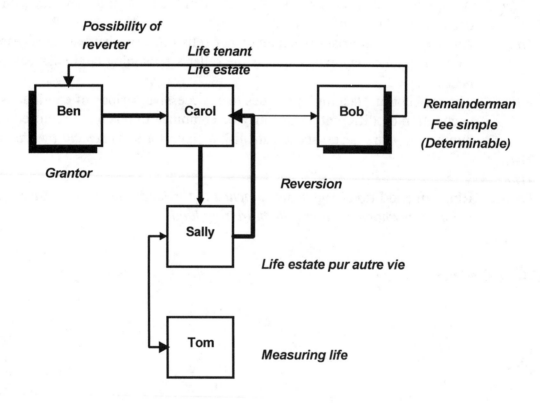

Figure 7.3 *Answers will vary, depending on state law*

Chapter 8

CHAPTER SUMMARY

1. severalty
2. tenancy in common
3. Joint tenancy
4. possession; interest; time; title
5. tenancy by the entirety
6. community property
7. trustor; trustee; beneficiary
8. cooperative
9. Condominium
10. Time-sharing

KEY TERM MATCHING, Part I

10 board of directors
3 joint tenancy
4 partition
8 partnership
9 proprietary lease
1 severalty
5 tenancy by the entirety
2 tenancy in common
7 testamentary trust
6 trust

KEY TERM MATCHING, Part II

7 assessments
8 condo fee
6 condominium
2 corporation
1 general partnership
3 joint venture
4 limited liability company
5 separate property
9 time-share estate
10 time-share use

TRUE AND FALSE

1. *True*
2. *False* The term "severalty" means that *there is one sole owner, who is severed or cut off from other owners.*
3. *False* In a *joint tenancy*, title is held as though all owners collectively constitute a single common unit, with the right of survivorship.
4. *True*
5. *False* A joint tenancy continues indefinitely, until there is only one remaining owner, who then holds title in *severalty.*
6. *True*
7. *False* The four unities characteristic of a *joint tenancy* are possession, interest, title and time.
8. *False* A joint tenant may freely convey his or her interest in the jointly held property to a new owner, *but doing so will destroy the unities of time and title and the new owner cannot become a joint tenant.*

9. *True*
10. *False* A tenancy by the entirety is a special form of ownership limited to married couples, *and title may be conveyed only by a deed signed by both parties: neither may convey a half-interest, and there is no right to partition or divide the property.*
11. *False* A tenancy by the entirety *may be terminated by divorce, agreement, court order or the death of one of the parties.*
12. *False* In a community property state, "community property" includes all property, both real and personal, acquired by either party *during* the marriage.
13. *True*
14. *False* In a *limited* partnership, the death of one of the officers does not affect the organization's continuity.
15. *False* When a corporation buys real property, the stockholders *do not have a direct ownership interest in the real estate because stock is personal property.*
16. *False* A *joint venture* is a form of partnership in which two or more people or firms carry out a single business project, with no intention of establishing an on-going or permanent relationship.
17. *False* Condominium owners hold their own units in fee simple and the common elements *as tenants in common.*
18. *True*
19. *True*
20. *False* A time-share estate is a *fee simple interest.*

MULTIPLE CHOICE

1.	b	6.	b
2.	c	7.	b
3.	a	8.	d
4.	c	9.	c
5.	b	10.	c

ILLUSTRATION

Figure 8.1

Condominium: Strike out *corporate ownership, occupancy and use for limited periods* and *proprietary lease*

Cooperative: Strike out *undivided interest in common elements, occupancy and use for limited periods* and *fee simple ownership of units*

Time-share: Strike out *corporate ownership* and *proprietary lease*

Chapter 9 ▌▌▌

CHAPTER SUMMARY

1. legal description
2. rectangular
3. metes-and-bounds
4. rectangular

5. township
6. 36
7. plat
8. datum

KEY TERM MATCHING

6 base lines
13 benchmarks
9 correction lines
12 datum
10 fractional sections
11 lot-and-block
1 metes-and-bounds

3 monuments
2 POB
5 principal meridians
8 ranges
4 rectangular survey system
7 township lines

TRUE AND FALSE

1. *False* The *rectangular survey system* was established by Congress in 1785.
2. *True*
3. *False* Principal meridians run *north and south*.
4. *True*
5. *False* *Ranges* are strips of land six miles wide that run parallel to the meridian.
6. *True*
7. *False* Each township contains 36 sections of *640* acres each.
8. *False* Section 6 is always in the *northwest* or upper left-hand corner.
9. *False* In the rectangular survey system, a comma may be used in place of the word *"of."*
10. *False* Areas smaller than a full quarter section are designated as *government lots*.
11. *False* A *benchmark* is a permanent reference point, usually found on an embossed brass marker set into a solid concrete or asphalt base, *used for marking datums*.
12. *True*

MULTIPLE CHOICE

1. b	4. b	7. c	10. b
2. b	5. b	8. a	11. a
3. b	6. c	9. c	12. d

Chapter 10 ▌▌▌

CHAPTER SUMMARY

1. lien
2. encumbrance
3. general
4. specific
5. voluntary
6. involuntary
7. equitable
8. priority
9. redeem
10. Special assessments

11. mortgage
12. mechanic's
13. judgment
14. attachment
15. lis pendens
16. inheritance
17. assets
18. general

KEY TERM MATCHING, Part I

10 ad valorem
 4 equitable lien
 5 general lien
 3 involuntary lien
 1 lien
 7 priority
 6 specific lien
 8 subordination
 9 taxes
 2 voluntary lien

KEY TERM MATCHING, Part II

 1 assessment
10 attachment
 2 equalization factor
 4 equitable right of redemption
 9 lis pendens
 7 mechanic's lien
 3 mill
 8 money judgment
 6 special assessments
 5 statutory right of redemption

TRUE AND FALSE

1. *False*   An *involuntary* lien may be classified as either statutory or equitable.
2. *True*
3. *False*   *Not* all encumbrances are liens.
4. *False*   Taking out a mortgage loan is an example of the creation of a *voluntary* lien.
5. *True*
6. *True*
7. *False*   A special assessment is always a specific and statutory lien, *but may be either involuntary or voluntary, depending on the nature of the improvement being funded.*
8. *False*   A court's decree that establishes the amount owed by a debtor is enforced by a

writ of execution directing the sheriff to seize and sell the debtor's property.

9. *True*
10. *False* "Ad valorem" *taxes are based on the value of the property being taxed.*
11. *True*
12. *True*
13. *True*
14. *False* A delinquent taxpayer may redeem property at any time prior to a tax sale by exercising his or her *equitable* right of redemption.
15. *True*

MULTIPLE CHOICE

1. d	4. b	7. c	10. c
2. b	5. c	8. d	11. a
3. c	6. a	9. c	12. a

ILLUSTRATION

Figure 10.1

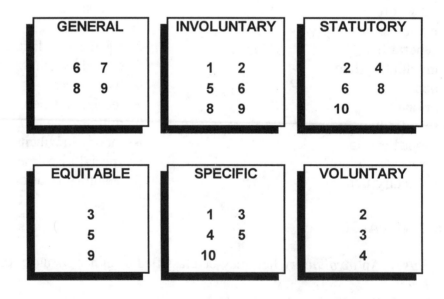

Chapter 11 ▌▌

CHAPTER SUMMARY

1. promise
2. express
3. bilateral
4. executed
5. executory

6. valid
7. novation
8. damages
9. option agreement
10. land

KEY TERM MATCHING, Part I

4 bilateral contract
10 consideration
1 contract
6 executed contract
7 executory contract
2 express contract
3 implied contract
9 mutual assent
8 offeree
5 unilateral contract

KEY TERM MATCHING, Part II

2 assignment
4 breach
9 contingencies
6 earnest money
7 equitable title
10 land contract
8 liquidated damages
5 listing agreement
3 novation
1 void

TRUE AND FALSE

1. *False* An agreement to be bound by *all* of the terms proposed in an offer constitutes acceptance.
2. *False* *While a contract may be written or oral, certain types of contracts must be in writing to be enforceable.*
3. *False* A listing agreement is *an employment contract between a broker and a seller.*
4. *True*
5. *False* In an implied contract, the actual agreement between the parties is *demonstrated by their acts and conduct.*
6. *False* The difference between a bilateral and a unilateral contract is the *presence or absence of the exchange of mutual promises.*
7. *True*
8. *False* A contract that may be rescinded or disaffirmed by one or both of the parties based on some legal principle is *voidable,* even though it may appear on the surface to be valid.

9. *False* The person who makes an offer is the *offeror*; the person who accepts or rejects the offer is the *offeree*.
10. *True*
11. *True*
12. *False* Under a land contract, the buyer obtains *possession but not title* to the property by agreeing to make regular monthly payments to the seller over a number of years.
13. *False* *Novation* is the substitution of a new contract in place of the original one, while *assignment* is a transfer of rights or duties under a contract
14. *True*
15. *False* An option contract is an agreement by which the *optionor* gives the *optionee* the right to buy or lease property at a fixed price within a specific period of time.
16. *True*
17. *True*
18. *True*
19. *True*
20. *False* A contract entered into by a minor is *voidable*.

MULTIPLE CHOICE

1. b
2. c
3. c
4. c
5. b

6. b
7. b
8. d
9. c
10. c

ILLUSTRATION

Figure 11.1

BUYER(S),_____
Address_____;
City _____State _____; Zip_____agrees to purchase, and
SELLER(S):__**PAUL PURVEYOR AND POLLY PURVEYOR**_____
Address:_**1105 AZALEA STREET**_____; City __**PLEASANT VALLEY__**
State_**EAST VIRGINIA___**; Zip __**98765**_____ agrees to sell to Buyer(s) at the
Price of_**ONE HUNDRED SEVENTEEN THOUSAND FIVE HUNDRED_** Dollars ($_**117,500_**)
the Property commonly described as **1105 AZALEA STREET**_____
(City of _**PLEASANT VALLEY**_____, County of _**POLEDUCK**_____,
State of _**EAST VIRGINIA**_____), "the Property," a complete legal
description of which may be attached to this contract by either party. The Property has
approximate lot dimensions of _**70 BY 160**_____, together with all existing

improvements and fixtures, if any, to be transferred to the Buyer(s) by Bill of Sale at the time of closing, including (but not limited to): hot water heater, furnace, plumbing and electrical fixtures, sump pumps, central heating and cooling, central heating and cooling systems, fixed floor coverings, built-in kitchen appliances and cabinets, storm and screen windows and doors, window treat-ment hardware, shelving systems, all planted vegetation, garage door openers and car units, and the following items of personal property:

KITCHEN STOVE, DISHWASHER, REFRIGERATOR;OUTDOOR GAS COOKER AND SWINGSET

2. EARNEST MONEY: Buyer has paid $_**17,625**_____ by check ~~by note~~ (circle one), and will pay within __**5**__ days the further sum of $_**9,9875.60**__, as earnest money to be applied against the purchase price. The earnest money shall be held by the Listing Broker for the mutual benefit of the parties. The balance of the purchase price, $_**89,887.50** shall be paid in full at closing.

3. CLOSING DATE: The closing date shall be _____, 19__, at _**LAW OFFICE OF R. TASSEL**

4. POSSESSION: Possession shall be at closing.

5. COMMISSION: Seller(s) agree that _**F.J. BROKER**_____, Listing Broker, brought about this sale and agrees to pay a Broker's commission as agreed in the listing agreement.

6. FINANCING: This contract is subject to the condition that Buyer(s) shall, by _____, 19 __, obtain a written commitment for a loan secured by a mortgage or deed of trust on the Property in the amount of $__**89, 887.50**_____. Financing shall be secured in the form of a mortgage of the following type:(delete those items that do not apply) Conventional (fixed ~~or adjustable rate~~); ~~FHA mortgage; VA mortgage; assumption of existing mortgage; financing by Seller(s)~~.

Chapter 12▐▐

CHAPTER SUMMARY

1. title
2. voluntary
3. acknowledged
4. granting
5. delivered
6. general warranty
7. special

8. bargain and sale
9. quitclaim
10. devise
11. Probate
12. accretion

KEY TERM MATCHING, Part I

7 acknowledgment
3 deed
10 deed in trust
5 grantee
6 granting clause
4 grantor
9 quiet enjoyment
8 seisin
1 title
2 voluntary alienation

KEY TERM MATCHING, Part II

2 bargain and sale
8 devise
6 involuntary alienation
10 probate
3 quitclaim
5 reconveyance deed
1 special warranty
7 testate
9 testator
4 trustee's deed

TRUE AND FALSE

1. *False* A title to real estate *is not an actual printed document.*
2. *True*
3. *False* To be valid, a deed must include a recital of consideration and an identifiable grantee*; a deed may contain a recital of exceptions and reservations.*
4. *False* A title is considered transferred when the deed is actually *delivered to the grantee by the grantor.*
5. *False* To be valid, a deed must be signed by *all grantors named in the deed.*
6. *False* In a *general* warranty deed, the covenant of seisin warrants that the grantor *is the owner of the property and has the right to convey it.*
7. *True*
8. *True*
9. *False* If a trustee wanted to convey real estate back to the grantor, he or she would use a *reconveyance deed.*
10. *True*
11. *True*
12. *False* When a property owner dies, his or her heirs by descent or will *immediately take title to the property, but may take possession only after probate.*
13. *True*
14. *True*
15. *False* Real property of an owner who dies intestate is distributed according to the laws of the state in which *the property is located.*

MULTIPLE CHOICE

1. b	4. c	7. a	10. b
2. c	5. b	8. d	11. c
3. d	6. b	9. c	12. c

ILLUSTRATIONS

Figure 12.1

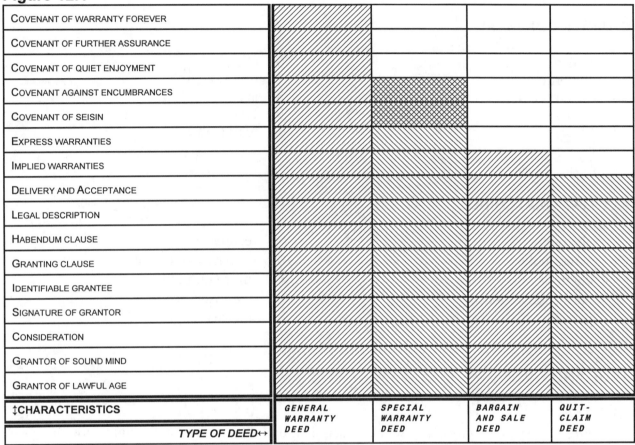

CHARACTERISTICS	GENERAL WARRANTY DEED	SPECIAL WARRANTY DEED	BARGAIN AND SALE DEED	QUIT-CLAIM DEED
COVENANT OF WARRANTY FOREVER	▨			
COVENANT OF FURTHER ASSURANCE	▨			
COVENANT OF QUIET ENJOYMENT	▨			
COVENANT AGAINST ENCUMBRANCES	▨	▨		
COVENANT OF SEISIN	▨	▨		
EXPRESS WARRANTIES	▨	▨		
IMPLIED WARRANTIES	▨	▨		
DELIVERY AND ACCEPTANCE	▨	▨	▨	▨
LEGAL DESCRIPTION	▨	▨	▨	▨
HABENDUM CLAUSE	▨	▨	▨	▨
GRANTING CLAUSE	▨	▨	▨	▨
IDENTIFIABLE GRANTEE	▨	▨	▨	▨
SIGNATURE OF GRANTOR	▨	▨	▨	▨
CONSIDERATION	▨	▨	▨	▨
GRANTOR OF SOUND MIND	▨	▨	▨	▨
GRANTOR OF LAWFUL AGE	▨	▨	▨	▨

TYPE OF DEED↔

NOTE: *The top two boxes of the* **special warranty deed** *bar indicate that its basic warranties are* similar *to the general warranty's covenants of seisin and against encumbrances. Remember that a special warranty deed contains TWO warranties: (1) that the grantor received title and (2) that the property was not encumbered during the time the grantor held it.*

Figure 12.2

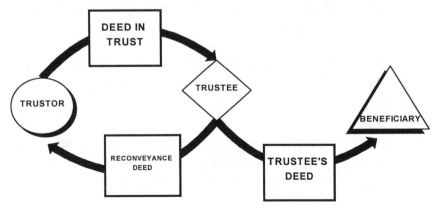

Chapter 13

CHAPTER SUMMARY

1. notice
2. Recording
3. constructive
4. actual
5. Priority

6. chain
7. title search
8. abstract
9. certificate
10. marketable

KEY TERM MATCHING

8   abstractor
3   actual notice
5   chain of title
2   constructive notice
4   priority

1   recording
10 security agreement
6   suit to quiet title
9   title insurance
7   title search

TRUE AND FALSE

1. *True*
2. *False*   *In most states,* any written document that affects any estate, right, title or interest in land must be recorded in the county *in which the property is located.*
3. *False*   To be eligible for recording, a document pertaining to real estate must be drawn and executed in accordance with the requirements of the *recording acts of the state in which the property is located.*
4. *False*   *Actual notice* means that the information about property is not only available, but that someone has been given access to that information.
5. *False*   A search of the public records will disclose all *recorded* liens that exist against a property.
6. *True*
7. *False*   In a typical title search, the chain of title is examined, *beginning with the present owner and tracing backwards to the earliest records of ownership.*
8. *True*
9. *True*
10. *False*   A certificate of title *is evidence of ownership, but not a guarantee.*
11. *False*   An *extended coverage* title insurance policy protects a homeowner against rights of parties in possession and unrecorded liens

12. *False*   The Torrens system is a legal registration system that is used in *fewer than ten states, most of which are in the process of phasing it out.*

MULTIPLE CHOICE

1. b	5. b
2. c	6. c
3. b	7. b
4. d	8. d

ILLUSTRATION

Figure 13.1

Barton Doyle and Jane Doyle	Anton Feldspar	Bargain and Sale Deed	March 7, 1940
Peter Parker and Mary Parker	Lamont Cranston and Gloria Reve	Warranty Deed	November 16, 1958

Peter and Mary Jane Parker conveyed as grantors, but there is no indication that they received title as grantees from Anton Feldspar.

Chapter 14 ▐

CHAPTER SUMMARY

1.	title	
2.	lien	
3.	intermediate	
4.	mortgage	
5.	Deed of trust	

6.	commitment
7.	note
8.	recorded
9.	release
10.	Default

KEY TERM MATCHING, Part I

10   acceleration clause
6   deed of trust
9   discount points
3   execute
5   hypothecation
7   interest
2   mortgagee
1   mortgagor
4   promissory note
8   usury

KEY TERM MATCHING, Part II

2   alienation clause
5   deed in lieu of foreclosure
1   defeasance clause
8   deficiency judgment
6   equitable right of redemption
4   foreclosure
7   statutory right of redemption
3   subordination agreement

TRUE AND FALSE

1. *False*   A mortgage is classified as a *voluntary* lien on real estate.
2. *False*   A mortgage is a two-party financing agreement in which a *mortgagor* pledges real property to the *mortgagee* as security for the debt.
3. *True*
4. *True*
5. *False*   The pledging of property as security for payment of a loan without actually surrendering possession of the property is referred to as *hypothecation*.
6. *True*
7. *True*
8. *False*   A point is 1 percent of *the amount being borrowed*.
9. *False*   *An acceleration clause* expedites foreclosure by giving a lender the right to declare the entire debt due and payable in the event of a borrower's default.
10. *True*
11. *False*   When a real estate loan secured by a deed of trust has been repaid in full, the trustee executes a *release deed* that releases the property back to the grantor.
12. *True*
13. *True*
14. *True*
15. *True*

MULTIPLE CHOICE

1. b
2. a
3. c
4. c
5. b
6. a
7. b
8. d
9. c
10. b
11. c
12. c

ILLUSTRATION

Figure 14.1

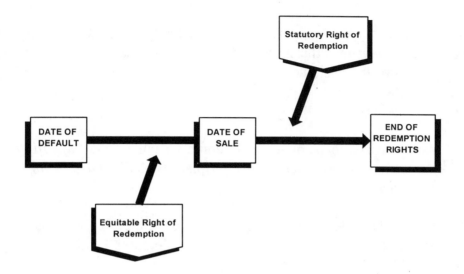

```
                                    ┌──────────────┐
                                    │ Statutory Right of │
                                    │  Redemption  │
                                    └──────────────┘
                                           │
                                           ▼
┌──────────┐         ┌──────────┐                    ┌──────────────┐
│ DATE OF  │────────▶│ DATE OF  │───────────────────▶│   END OF     │
│ DEFAULT  │         │  SALE    │                    │ REDEMPTION   │
└──────────┘         └──────────┘                    │   RIGHTS     │
              ▲                                       └──────────────┘
              │
       ┌──────────────┐
       │ Equitable Right of │
       │   Redemption  │
       └──────────────┘
```

Chapter 15 |||

CHAPTER SUMMARY

1. Federal Reserve Board
2. secondary
3. straight
4. amortized
5. index

6. loan-to-value
7. purchase-money
8. FHA; VA
9. Regulation Z; Truth-in-Lending
10. computerized loan origination (CLO)

KEY TERM MATCHING, Part I

10 amortized loan
1   Federal Reserve
4   fiduciary lenders
7   FNMA
8   GNMA
5   mortgage brokers
3   primary mortgage market
2   prime rate
6   secondary mortgage market
9   straight loan

KEY TERM MATCHING, Part II

1   adjustable-rate mortgage
6   buydown
3   certificate of eligibility
2   growing-equity mortgage
5   package loan
4   purchase-money mortgage

TRUE AND FALSE

1. *False*   The *primary mortgage market* is made up of the lenders who originate loans.
2. *False*   The *prime rate* is the short-term interest rate charged to a bank's largest, most credit-worthy customers.
3. *True*
4. *True*
5. *True*
6. *False*   An amortized loan applies each monthly payment *first toward the interest owed on the loan; the remainder of each payment is then applied toward paying off the principal amount.*
7. *True*
8. *False*   In an adjustable rate mortgage, the *adjustment period* establishes how often the rate may be changed.
9. *True*
10. *False*   The "value" portion of a property's LTV is the *lower* of the sale price or the appraised value.
11. *True*
12. *False*   *Like the FHA*, the VA *does not make* purchase-money loans to qualified individuals.
13. *False*   A *blanket* loan covers more than one parcel or lot, and is usually used to finance subdivision developments.
14. *True*
15. *True*
16. *False*   *Under Regulation Z, a borrower other than a residential purchase-money or first mortgage borrower* has three days in which to rescind a transaction simply by notifying the lender of his or her intent to rescind.
17. *False*   Under the Community Reinvestment Act, the findings of the government agency review of an institution's community reinvestment activities *must be made public.*
18. *False*   A computerized loan origination system allows a real estate broker to *assist a buyer in selecting a lender and applying for a loan.*

MULTIPLE CHOICE

1. a		9. b	
2. b		10. d	
3. b		11. c	
4. b		12. c	
5. b		13. b	
6. c		14. a	
7. c		15. b	
8. c		16. b	

ILLUSTRATION

Figure 15.1

TYPE OF LOAN	PURCHASE PRICE	MAXIMUM LOAN	DOWN PAYMENT	P&I PER MONTH
80% CONVENTIONAL	$92,000	$73,600	$18,400	$540.22
90% CONVENTIONAL	$92,000	$82,800	$ 9,200	$607.75
FHA	$92,000	$87,900	$ 4,100	$645.00
VA	$92,000	$92,000	$ 0	$675.28

Chapter 16 ▌▌▌

CHAPTER SUMMARY

1. lease
2. estate; years
3. from period to period
4. at will
5. at sufferance
6. personal
7. contract
8. terminated
9. constructive eviction
10. Americans with Disabilities

KEY TERM MATCHING

11 actual eviction
8 assignment
12 constructive eviction
1 lease
3 leasehold
10 option

5 periodic tenancy
2 reversionary right
9 sublease
7 tenancy at sufferance
6 tenancy at will
4 tenancy for years

TRUE AND FALSE

1. *False* In a lease agreement, the landlord is the *lessor* and the tenant is the *lessee*.
2. *True*
3. *False* Although an extension of a tenancy for years requires a new contract, the lease may be terminated prior to the expiration date *only if both parties agree or if one party has breached the agreement*.
4. *True*
5. *True*
6. *True*
7. *True*
8. *True*
9. *True*
10. *False* Under a *gross* lease agreement, the landlord pays all the operating expenses of the property, while the tenant pays only a fixed rental.
11. *True*
12. *True*
13. *False* To be entitled to constructive eviction, the tenant must show only that the premises have become unusable for the purpose stated in the lease *due to the landlord's conscious neglect*.
14. *True*

MULTIPLE CHOICE

1. d
2. d
3. c
4. d
5. a
6. c

7. d
8. b
9. b
10. c
11. b
12. c

ILLUSTRATION

Figure 16.1

Acrylic Acres has a *net lease*, with $2,902.50 rent for the current month.

Blue Buttons Boutique has a *gross lease*, with $2,000 rent for the current month.

Custom Custards has a *percentage lease*, with $2,515 rent for the current month.

Chapter 17

CHAPTER SUMMARY

1. income
2. agent
3. management agreement
4. rent
5. Maintenance

6. insurance
7. Fire and hazard
8. Casualty
9. public liability
10. Worker's compensation

KEY TERM MATCHING

10 audit
8 casualty
9 consequential loss
2 life cycle costing
1 management agreement

7 multiperil
3 preventive maintenance
5 risk management
6 surety bond
4 tenant improvements

TRUE AND FALSE

1. *True*
2. *False* The management agreement creates a *general* agency relationship between an owner and the property manager.
3. *False* *Like* real estate brokers' commissions, property management fees *may not be standardized by local associations, but must be negotiated between the parties.*
4. *True*
5. *False* *A high vacancy rate, by itself, does not prove that rent is too high.*
6. *False* The manager of a *commercial* building should carefully consider a prospective tenant's compatibility with existing tenants.
7. *False* A high tenant turnover rate results in *lower* profits for the owner.
8. *True*
9. *False* *Preventive* maintenance helps prevent problems and expenses before they arise.
10. *False* Tenant improvements are major alterations to the interior of commercial or industrial property, *usually performed by the property manager.*
11. *False* Under *Title III* of the ADA, *existing barriers must be removed from commercial properties when this can be accomplished in a readily achievable manner.*
12. *True*
13. *True*

14. *False*   In a commercial property, the risk of a shopper suffering a slip-and-fall injury would be covered by *liability insurance*.

15. *False*   A building is insured for what it would cost to rebuild it in a *current replacement cost policy*.

MULTIPLE CHOICE

1. c
2. d
3. c
4. c
5. d

6. d
7. c
8. c
9. d
10. c

ILLUSTRATION

Figure 17.1

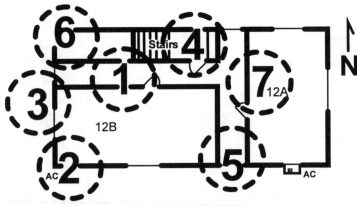

1: Paint 12th floor east-west hallway   **PREVENTIVE**

2: Fix air conditioner in 12B: blows hot   **CORRECTIVE**

3: Tuckpoint exterior brick on west side   **PREVENTIVE**

4: Replace stained carpet on stair landing   **CORRECTIVE**

5: Repair cracked window, hallway-south   **ROUTINE**

6: Annual elevator inspection and repair   **PREVENTIVE**

7: Reverse 12A entry door to open in;   **CONSTRUCTION**
   widen doorway and replace door to
   accommodate tenant in wheelchair

Chapter 18

CHAPTER SUMMARY

1. appraisal
2. market value
3. economic
4. Value
5. Cost
6. Price

7. sales comparison
8. cost
9. income
10. gross rent multiplier
11. gross income multiplier
12. reconciliation

KEY TERM MATCHING, Part I

5 anticipation
1 appraisal
2 appraiser
10 assemblage
6 change
7 conformity
8 contribution
9 highest and best use
4 market value
3 transferability

KEY TERM MATCHING, Part II

7 cost approach
10 depreciation
11 economic life
12 income approach
1 plottage
3 progression
2 regression
9 replacement cost
8 reproduction cost
6 sales comparison
4 substitution
5 supply and demand

TRUE AND FALSE

1. *False* Title XI of FIRREA requires that all residential property *valued at $250,000 or more in a federally related transaction be appraised by a state licensed or certified appraiser.*
2. *True*
3. *False* The market *price* of a property is what it actually sells for in an open market transaction.
4. *False* Cost and market value *may be, but are not necessarily, the same.*
5. *True*
6. *True*
7. *True*
8. *False* The economic principle of *substitution* holds that the maximum value of a property tends to be set by the cost of purchasing a similarly desirable property.

9. *False* In the sales comparison approach to value, a feature that is present in the subject property but not present in a comparable property is *added* to the sales price of the comparable.
10. *True*
11. *True*
12. *True*
13. *False* The income approach to value is based on the *present* value of the rights to *future* income.
14. *True*
15. *False* Reconciliation involves *a detailed and professional analysis and application of the three approaches to value, not simply an average of the different results.*

MULTIPLE CHOICE

1.	b	7.	b
2.	b	8.	c
3.	b	9.	c
4.	d	10.	c
5.	d	11.	c
6.	b	12.	b

ILLUSTRATION

Figure 18.1

1. 1234
2. 1238 lowers the value of 1236 and 1234
3. 1236 raises the value of 1234 and 1238
4. Anticipation

5. Declined
6. Conformity
7. Contribution

||Chapter 19

CHAPTER SUMMARY

1. direct public ownership
2. enabling acts; police powers
3. Comprehensive plans
4. Zoning ordinances
5. Building codes
6. public
7. subdivider

8. developer
9. master plans
10. subdivision
11. plat
12. Clustering
13. restrictions; covenants
14. interstate

KEY TERM MATCHING, Part I

5 buffer zones
6 bulk zoning
1 comprehensive plan
9 conditional-use permit
4 enabling acts
2 master plan
8 nonconforming use
7 taking
10 variance
3 zoning ordinances

KEY TERM MATCHING, Part II

7 building codes
1 building permit
5 density zoning
3 developer
4 plat
6 restrictive covenants
2 subdivider

TRUE AND FALSE

1. *False* The *comprehensive plan* creates the broad, general framework for a community; *zoning ordinances* define the details and implement the plan.

2. *False* *Incentive zoning* is used to ensure that certain types of uses are incorporated into developments.

3. *False* Property owners are protected against the unreasonable or arbitrary taking of their land by the takings clause of the *Fifth* Amendment to the United States Constitution.

4. *True*

5. *False* A *variance* allows a landowner to use his or her property in a manner that is otherwise strictly prohibited by the existing zoning.

6. *False* A property owner who wants to build a structure or alter or repair an existing building usually must first obtain a *building* permit.

7. *True*

8. *True*

9. *False* A detailed map that illustrates the geographic boundaries of individual lots is called a *plat*.

10. *True*

11. *False* A restrictive covenant is considered a reasonable, legal restraint if it protects property values and *does not restrict the free transfer of property.*

12. *False* The Interstate Land Sales Full Disclosure Act requires *developers of certain unimproved property offered in interstate commerce by telephone or through the mail* to file a disclosure statement with HUD.

MULTIPLE CHOICE

1. c
2. d
3. b
4. b
5. d
6. c

7. c
8. c
9. c
10. b
11. a

ILLUSTRATION

Figure 19.1

1. J-9 is in the *commercial* zone; J-8 may be used for *residential* development; K8 is limited to *industrial* use.
2. *conditional use permit*
3. *J-1 through J-8* (a park would serve the residential neighborhoods and provide a buffer between the residential and industrial zones).
4. The rezoning could be a *takings* issue if the value of the property is decreased.
5. The house is a *nonconforming use*. It was most likely *grandfathered in*.
6. One *possible* location would be the square bounded by J-7, G-7, G-9 and J-9: it would provide retail services near the residential neighborhood, professional services near the commercial zone, and would not be disruptive to the industrial zone. Other possibilities include A-8 through F-8, or six units between J-1 and J-8 as a buffer. It would probably *not* be wise to place the new zone in the center of the residential area (due to traffic and noise), or in the industrial zone (it could present hazards to shoppers).

▌▌▌Chapter 20

CHAPTER SUMMARY

1. Fair Housing Act
2. disciplinary action
3. familial status
4. disability
5. reasonable accommodations

6. Intentional
7. HUD
8. redlining
9. Ethics
10. code of ethics